DISTINCTIVE DISCIPLESHIP

BIBLE STUDY

DISTINCTIVE DISCIPLESHIP

Designing Specific Plans for Christian Maturity

BIBLE STUDY

TRAVIS AGNEW

DISTINCTIVE DISCIPLESHIP BIBLE STUDY

ISBN: 9781086607598

TABLE OF CONTENTS

INTRODUCTION

For all those who feel stuck in their spiritual life, you don't have to accept stagnation as the norm any longer. In this 8-week Bible study, I want to walk you through a model called Distinctive Discipleship. It attempts to encourage individual people with particular needs to develop a unique plan for a given season. You can use this model within the church house, coffee house, or your house. It can be implemented by a mentor, a leader of a small group, or by a parent. The process is not contingent upon a particular context, and any believer in any nation in the world can apply its simple principles. This model will be good for an individual, better with a partner, but best with a mentor.

The guide within these pages will help you create a plan for discipleship in your individual context. If every Christian is in a unique place surrounded by specific challenges, why do we think that a broad approach will work for every single one of us? We don't need ministry templates; we need distinctive discipleship. Each person is too complex for generalized approaches to meet all of our needs.

The desperate need for discipleship seems to be a cyclical point of conversation within our churches. Every so often, we begin to notice the warning signs concerning the overarching lack of spiritual maturity among the majority of believers, and we seem emphatically determined to address it. Upon these alarming realizations, we speak very poignantly regarding the need for discipleship by criticizing those before us who apparently did an insufficient job.

Instead of belaboring points of why specific ministries failed to prioritize discipleship in the past, I think it is a wiser use of our time to activate the church around us for discipleship in the present. Let's return to the simple paths of discipleship encouraged and exemplified within the pages of Scripture and make a valiant effort to imitate it. Instead of providing a plan that might be overwhelming to implement, let's simplify to a process that is easily memorizable, adaptable, and repeatable. I want to make it simple, engaging, and distinctive. Let's make disciples.

IF YOU ARE STUDYING SOLO

You can finish this study on your own. This resource was designed so that it doesn't require a leader book to unlock extra content. I do recommend for you to consider the need to allow someone into this process alongside you. If your spiritual life has lacked a specific direction for growth, any plan is better than no plan. Developing a particular strategy on your own is far better than accepting spiritual apathy as the normative experience. My experience reveals that this process is good for an individual, better with a partner, but best with a mentor. Even if you go through the study solo, please consider either an accountability partner or a personal mentor to help you during and after the process.

IF YOU ARE LEADING A GROUP

This study was designed to provide you enough content to study and discuss, but it also was crafted in such a way to bring your unique perspective to your specific group. As you prepare to teach the sections, provide your distinct illustrations and unique examples. Depending upon the size of your group, decide which activities are done as a whole group, within smaller groups, or on an individual basis. Note that this study might differ from other studies in the fact that once the eight weeks are complete, the work really begins. While your group might start right into another study, the whole premise of this one focuses on a 6-12 month implementation time after the study concludes. Consider how to establish opportunities for accountability once the sessions are complete.

ADDITIONAL RESOURCES

In addition to this Bible study workbook, I did write a standalone book on this concept. I believe in this process so much that I wanted to provide it in multiple formats. You do not need to read the book to do this study, but if you decide to do so, each session has chapters that naturally connect and are provided within the week's lesson. I also have a collection of sermons, podcast episodes, articles, and downloads of further resources at travisagnew.org/distinctive.

SESSION 1

EVALUATING
DISTINCTION

*Him we proclaim, warning everyone and teaching everyone with
all wisdom, that we may present everyone mature in Christ (Col. 1:28).*

Generalized approaches can never adequately address distinct disciples. If someone has never expressed this thought to you before, you need to be aware – you are entirely unique. Some people can relate to you, but no one is exactly like you. In order to see legitimate discipleship take place in your life and in the lives of those around you, we cannot depend upon widespread methods hoping to address the specific needs of everyone. It is time to get distinct in your discipleship.

CONSIDER

As you sit and read this page, you arrived at this specific location by some path. You might be meeting on your church campus, inside a home, or at some other gathering place, but you used some means of transportation to arrive where you are seated right now. Imagine that someone wanted to join you and asked you this simple question: "Can you tell me how to get to your Bible study next week?"

To help guide your friend, what is the next question you must ask?

You cannot give directions to a person without knowing his or her starting place. None of us can help someone arrive at a destination without first knowing the place of origin.

Answer the following questions and share them with the group:

1. **Did you take a left or a right out of your driveway to get here?**
2. **How many minutes did it take you to get here?**
3. **What road did you travel on for the majority of the trip?**
4. **Was this building on the left side or the right side of the road when you approached?**

We all got to the same place, but we didn't come by the same path. The same is true with discipleship. If the gospel of Jesus Christ has changed you, your glorified destination is none other than heaven, but your sanctified trajectory will be different from those around you.

Now answer these following questions and share them with the group:

1. **Who first introduced you to Jesus?**

2. **How many years have you been following Jesus?**

3. **What made you desire to join this study?**

4. **What kind of turn do you hope to make in your spiritual journey?**

Even in these simple questions, we process a simple truth – we are all in a different place spiritually. We each have unique turns that we need to make in the near future. So, let's begin to discover the next set of directions.

STUDY

As Jesus ascended into heaven, he provided simple instructions for his disciples to go and make more disciples (Matt. 28:18-20). By imitating his example, they were to take everything they had learned from Jesus and to pass it on to others. Within the first few chapters of the Book of Acts, we see that the disciples, now empowered by the Holy Spirit (Acts 2:4), were ready for such a task. On one particular day, Peter and John went to the temple to pray and healed a lame beggar in the name of Jesus (Acts 3:6).

The response of the beggar and the reaction of the crowd indicated that Jesus' ministry had been multiplied through these disciples. Just like Jesus, the presence of a favorable crowd always meant that the critics weren't too far behind. Have someone in the group read Acts 4:1-13 to see what happened next.

If you know the character of Peter while Jesus was on earth, what makes his speech at this occasion so surprising?

What makes Acts 4:13 so important for our understanding of discipleship (consider the negative assumptions and the positive descriptions)?

Peter and John were different people. After three years of discipleship, Jesus had forever left them with his imprint. They reminded people of Jesus. What a goal for all of us!

Not only did Jesus make a complete difference in the disciples, but he also made a specific change in each one of them. Look up the verses below as a group, or give out specific assignments. Write down indications of who they were before and after discipleship.

	Peter	John
Pre-Discipleship	Matt. 16:21-23; 26:69-75	Mark 3:17; 9:38-41
	John 18:10	Luke 9:51-56
Post-Discipleship	Acts 5:27-32	John 19:26-27
	1 Pet. 2:21	1 John 4:7-8

What a difference three years with Jesus can make. Peter, who was at first adamant about resisting suffering, established that as the major theme of his later writings. John, who was at first resistant to show compassion to others, is later marked by tender love. Do you think that these character traits just developed by accident? Or do you believe Jesus saw the need where these disciples were and started working on each one intentionally?

If you studied the unique contributions of Philip, Thomas, and other disciples, you might be surprised to see Jesus working individually with each one regarding different issues. His goal was holiness for all of them, but they each had distinct obstacles towards that goal. Jesus employed specific approaches for each one of them, and they each later were recognized as having been with Jesus himself (Acts 4:13).

DISCUSS

So, where did Jesus find you? What has he been working on intentionally? Take a moment and make some bullet points of the most essential elements in your spiritual life thus far. These items can be people, places, trips, or events. They can be positive or negative.

Take a few minutes to write down the significant pieces of your faith story.

Now that you have written down those items, categorize what they are. Typically, the points on your list will fall into one of the following six categories. Read through the list, and then identify to which category each item belongs. Write out the word or use the symbol accompanying each item.

1. **Event** - Do you have a milestone when God changed your life?

2. **Environment** - What regular faith gatherings shaped who you are today?

3. **Equipment** - What spiritual disciplines trained you to grow in godliness?

4. **Engagement** - How did you intentionally invest in another with what you learned?

5. **Encourager** - Who is that friend or friends who walked beside you and pushed you towards Christ?

6. **Example** - Who is the example you aspired to follow?

As a group, discuss what this exercise revealed to you. You probably will not have enough time to unpack every item, but is there something significant that you realized? Was there something pivotal for you? Is there something you know you have been lacking?

EVALUATE

By now, you are hopefully starting to realize that we are all unique people with specific spiritual needs. That's why we each need to design a specific plan for Christian maturity. You can accomplish this through a process called Distinctive Discipleship.

The origin of the model comes from the Apostle Paul's instructions to the Colossian church. As he instructed these believers, he taught concerning the amazing riches of beholding the glory of Jesus. In Colossians 1, he provided the framework that we will be using.

> *To them God chose to make known how great among the Gentiles are the riches of the glory of this mystery, which is Christ in you, the hope of glory. Him we proclaim, warning everyone and teaching everyone with all wisdom, that we may present everyone mature in Christ. For this I toil, struggling with all his energy that he powerfully works in me (Col. 1:27-29).*

Within these three verses, we find six guiding principles with which to make disciples:

1. **Delight** - *Christ in you, the hope of glory* - Discipleship must be motivated by the wondrous delight of knowing Jesus.

2. **Disobedience** - *warning everyone* - Discipleship must warn against disobedience in any sinful leanings specific to the individual.

3. **Doctrine** - *teaching everyone with all wisdom* - Discipleship must wisely equip the follower to possess increasingly competent biblical doctrine.

4. **Development** - *present everyone mature in Christ* - Discipleship must address areas of calling with the intention to bring about ministry development.

5. **Discipline** - *for this I toil* - Discipleship must train in areas of spiritual discipline for continual growth.

6. **Dependence** - *struggling with all his energy that he powerfully works in me* - Discipleship must continually acknowledge the complete dependence upon Jesus for the believer's maturity.

By utilizing these six categories, you are going to design a specific plan for Christian maturity. While each person will use these categories, each plan will be uniquely dependent upon the given person's situation.

SHARE

In the next few weeks, you will develop a thorough Distinctive Discipleship plan. While these categories may present some questions in your mind, the designations should be enough to get your mind thinking right away.

Is there a particular category that you are most eager to address? With the group, share your answer and why. Protect confidentiality with what others share in this group.

At the end of this study, you will not be a perfect disciple, but you will be on the way to making progress. Could you share with the group what your prayer would be for your spiritual condition by the end of this study?

SESSION NOTES

If you are reading the ***Distinctive Discipleship*** book to accompany this study, read **chapters 1-3** before coming to the group next time. Don't worry – while the book will allow you to develop these concepts fuller, this workbook is sufficient to lead you through the process.

MAKE DISCIPLES – NOT CONVERTS

"Go therefore and make disciples..."
(Matt. 28:19).

Jesus instructed in the Great Commission for his disciples to go and make more disciples. He spent almost every hour of three years with twelve men. Through his instruction and example, those remaining knew how to pass along everything they had to others who would go and do the same. The fact that you are reading this book indicates that the process is working!

Read Jesus' parting words to his disciples in Matt. 28:16-20. As you read, notice the description of what he called them to do.

Write out answers to the following questions.

Jesus instructed them to make disciples. What do you think is the difference between a disciple and a convert?

How does the standard of "teaching them to observe all that I commanded" differ from the expectations we often have of discipleship?

Jesus wanted disciples – not converts. He discipled men who would continue to grow, not just men who would maintain an undeveloped faith. Pray that God would help you understand the need for discipleship in your life and in how you should invest in others.

DAY 2: INVESTIGATE

FISHERS OF MEN

"Follow me, and I will make you fishers of men."
(Matt. 4:19).

It is never an ordinary day when Jesus shows up to your job. In the initial stages of Jesus' ministry, his reputation was spreading quickly. This man was no regular rabbi. He was not a humdrum holy man. When he interrupted your life, you would eventually thank him for it.

Read what happened when Jesus called some of his first disciples in Matthew 4:18-25.

Jesus was a carpenter by trade (Mark 6:3), and he dared to ask some fishermen to change their profession while he taught them how to do it. Jesus never asked Matthew the tax-collector to become a fisher of men. **While the reasoning is obvious, what does his method show us about Jesus willingness to use our distinct context?**

Would Jesus ask you to be a fisher of men or something else? Based on the focus of your life, what would Jesus ask you to do?

Think about all that these disciples watched Jesus do (4:23-25). They could have missed it by refusing to leave their comfortable boats. As Jesus calls you further into discipleship, what are you hoping you see him do? What are you hoping that he teaches you?

DAY 3: IMITATE

4 STAGES OF DISCIPLESHIP

And immediately they left their nets and followed him
(Mark 1:18).

While there are many examples of how Jesus trained his disciples, we are limited in our exposure. With them spending three years with him, they experienced countless lessons and experiences of which we are unfortunately unaware. Jesus did so much in his life that the world is unable to contain all the volumes that they could have written about him (John 21:25).

Among all the events of which we do know, we notice that he gradually gave the disciples more responsibility. Over time, he expected more out of them based upon his training. Jesus followed this simple progression: 1) I do it, and you watch, 2) I do it, and you help, 3) you do it, and I help, and 4) you do it, and I watch. Read the following passages. Beside each one, write out how it depicts that moment in the progression.

1. **I Do It, and You Watch** - Luke 6:12-19

2. **I Do It, and You Help** - Luke 9:10-17

3. **You Do It, and I Help** - Luke 9:37-43

4. **You Do It, and I Watch** - Luke 10:1-12, 17-20

Have you ever had someone teach you as Jesus did? Have you ever taught someone like this? Now is the time to begin this progression. Pray for an opportunity today to follow this example in one tangible way.

DENY YOURSELF

*"If anyone would come after me, let him deny himself
and take up his cross and follow me" (Mark 8:34).*

Jesus never lacked clarity. He did not want to leave his disciples unsure of the
level of commitment needed to follow him. In one of his most blunt explanations,
he raised the bar regarding discipleship. Read his words in Mark 8:34-38.

Did you notice that he called two different groups of people at the beginning of
this scene? What are the words used, and how would you define each one (8:34)?

1.

2.

Before Jesus gave these words, he called the crowd and the disciples. Plenty of
people showed interest in being associated with Jesus, but few actually followed
him. If anyone wanted to join that group, he made it very clear regarding the
degree of devotion.

How is discipleship related to denying yourself?

**How could certain attempts at saving one's life (protecting comforts
and conveniences) potentially ruin discipleship efforts?**

GOOD SOLDIERS

No soldier gets entangled in civilian pursuits,
since his aim is to please the one who enlisted him (2 Tim. 2:4).

Sightseeing is never a luxury of wartime living. Soldiers embattled in a foreign land never take lavish tours. They know that they came for a mission and purposeless activity wasn't the goal. Read Paul's vivid description in 2 Timothy 2:1-7 of how that essential mindset should be present in the life of a disciple.

Paul mentored Timothy, and he expected Timothy to entrust all that his discipleship entailed into the lives of others who would go and do the same. Who has mentored you? Who have you mentored or have the potential to mentor? In the space below, write down the top 3 for each category.

PERSONAL MENTORS   **POTENTIAL MENTEES**

What type of "civilian pursuits" (2:4) could distract your discipleship?

Since Jesus has "enlisted" you, how will you make it your aim to please him today?

DISTINCTION REVIEW

To review this week, have you acknowledged where you are spiritually and processed where you need to be?

Generalized approaches will never adequately address distinctive disciples.

1. How would you describe your spiritual condition right now?

2. Where do you think you should be by this point in your life?

3. In which areas do you believe that you have the most potential to grow?

4. If the goal is an increasing level of spiritual maturity, write out a simple prayer for what you hope the Spirit does in your life during this study.

PLAN NOTES

SESSION 2

DISCOVERING DELIGHT

"Because you did not serve the LORD your God with joyfulness and gladness of heart, because of the abundance of all things" (Deut. 28:47).

What is the difference between a person who serves Jesus out of duty versus one who follows him out of delight? The implications are massively important. If you develop a Distinctive Discipleship plan because it is what you should do rather than what you get to do, the difference will eventually show. To address the first category in your plan, you must discover the necessary delight to invigorate discipleship.

CONSIDER

Each of us has things in our lives we embrace doing and other tasks we avoid doing. What is your list? Write down three items and reasons for each column and share them with the group.

	Embrace Doing	Why?
1		
2		
3		

	Avoid Doing	Why?
1		
2		
3		

What did you notice about your tasks? You probably discovered that you anticipate rewards with what you embrace and yet doubt the worth of successful completion with those tasks you avoid. You will do hard things if you want something bad enough. Even if an assignment is challenging, you will approach it with joy if you value the benefit of accomplishment greater than the burden of the effort.

When it comes to discipleship, the entire plan rises and falls on how you view the process. The most critical question to answer right now is: **Why do you want to grow in Christ?**

Session 2 of Distinctive Discipleship is all about discovering delight. If we revisit Colossians 1, Paul wrote, "To them God chose to make known how great among the Gentiles are the riches of the glory of this mystery, which is Christ in you, the hope of glory. Him we proclaim..." (Col. 1:27-28). If we can truly comprehend that the fullness of God dwelt in Christ (Col. 1:19), and now the fullness of Christ dwells in us (Col. 1:27), it should cause us to become overwhelmed with a joy that energizes our desire to take advantage of that blessed nearness.

STUDY

A rich young man wanted to follow Jesus, but he loved his possessions too much. Like him, we all have something that could rob us of following Jesus because we cherish that component too much. Owning something and being owned by something are two completely different things. Read what happened in Mark 10:17-22.

While this man had everything that the world had to offer, he was concerned about what would happen when he died. Having everything in this life doesn't guarantee your standing for eternal life. His mind turned to eternal matters, and so he wisely questioned the most popular spiritual guru of his day.

In reading Scripture, it is always helpful to determine the context of what is happening before and after a particular passage. **Why do you think this event is recorded right after what happens in Mark 10:13-16?**

After Jesus welcomed eager children into his presence, he was approached by an inquisitive professional who walked away from his presence. The children were mesmerized by Jesus, but this rich man was unfortunately too enamored with his possessions. These youth were wanting to come to Jesus (Mark 10:14), and this rich man was attempting to prove he had been morally upright since he was a youth (Mark 10:20).

In Mark 10:21, don't miss the description of Jesus. As Jesus focuses on this rich man, somehow onlookers can discern his legitimate love for him. In the most pivotal moment of this rich man's life, Jesus lovingly said the most challenging piece of information that he had ever heard: "You lack one thing: go, sell all that you have and give to the poor, and you will have treasure in heaven; and come, follow me" (Mark 10:21).

We don't see Jesus make this request to every person he encounters. What is the weight of that statement to this specific man?

What does Jesus' unique approach show us about his strategy?

Jesus' request wasn't a prerequisite – it was an assessment. His response revealed his commitment. Jesus already loved him, but this man didn't love Jesus. He wanted his stuff more than he wanted Jesus.

"Disheartened by the saying, he went away sorrowful, for he had great possessions" (Mark 10:22). This man forsook heavenly treasures for earthly treasures. Most likely, he left this encounter and continued to invest in what he wanted most of all. He never followed Jesus because he found delight in something more.

DISCUSS

While money is a significant deterrent for many people seeking to follow Jesus, there are many other culprits out there as well. Some of them can even be good things until they turn into god things.

What are some of the most significant distractions from following Jesus in our culture? Write down your list and share them as a group.

Out of all of these mentioned, which ones present the most significant amount of concern for you personally? Circle 2-3 that could distract you from following Jesus. If you don't see your issues, feel free to add items that endanger you.

The most critical element in your discipleship is to make Jesus both your priority and your privilege.

What does a disciple look like when making Jesus the priority?

What is unique about a person who follows Jesus as a privilege?

If you had to describe your devotion to Jesus now, would you say it is more of an obligation or an opportunity? Give yourself a score and explain why you selected that number to the group.

| 1 | 2 | 3 | 4 | 5 | 6 | 7 | 8 | 9 | 10 |

OBLIGATION   **OPPORTUNITY**

While much of the Christian life requires a resolved commitment to remain faithful, we also need more than apathetic submission. We might be guilty of doing the right thing but doing it in the wrong way. If our devotion isn't motivated by a delight of the possibility of knowing Jesus more, we will eventually stall out in our efforts. Have you forgotten the wondrous privilege it is to know him in the first place?

Think of a scenario where a person offers a generous gift while lacking a sincere eagerness to give it. Share a possible way that could happen.

What would be wrong with such an offering?

How does that relate to our potential desires of following Jesus?

God once chastised his people not for doing the wrong thing, but for doing the right thing in the wrong way. "Because you did not serve the LORD your God with joyfulness and gladness of heart, because of the abundance of all things, therefore you shall serve your enemies whom the LORD will send against you" (Deut. 28:47-48). Their abundance in prosperity was stealing their joy in what should have been their one genuine delight.

EVALUATE

The Israelites were guilty of delighting in the gifts rather than the Giver. The rich young man valued the treasures of this world rather than the treasure of the heavens. What about you? If someone watched you over the last month, what would they suspect could be the greatest delight of your life? These might be unhelpful habits, healthy relationships, or even religious activities. **Write down 1-3 possibilities.**

Why would they think you prioritize those items so much?

If you are obsessed with acquiring satisfaction from something other than Jesus, you might have uncovered a potential god in your life. The only way to put Jesus in the proper place is by dethroning that rival god and discovering delight in your relationship with the one true God.

What are some ways that you might have to work towards that end?

SHARE

In your group, share your discovery. **What is attempting to replace Jesus as your greatest joy?**

How will you discover delight in the fact you get to grow closer to Jesus?

Allow volunteers to locate the following verses and read them aloud to one another. Listen for the importance of joy being the stimulus for growth.

Ps. 37:4	**Jn. 15:11**	**Phil. 1:25**	**Ps. 16:11**	**1 Pet. 1:8**
Phil. 3:8	**2 Cor. 1:24**	**Matt. 13:44**	**Ps. 90:14**	**Jer. 15:16**

It's time to put this to work in your plan. Pray that God will guide you to discover an authentic delight in the privilege of knowing him.

SESSION NOTES

If you are reading the ***Distinctive Discipleship*** book to accompany this study, read **chapters 4-5** before coming to the group next time.

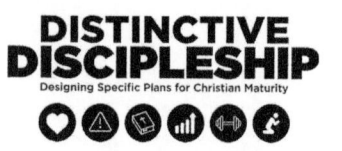

GOLDEN DISTRACTIONS

*"They have turned aside quickly out of the way that I commanded them.
They have made for themselves a golden calf..." (Ex. 32:8)*

God's miraculous deliverance was short-lived in the minds of the Israelites. As Moses lingered in the presence of the LORD on Mt. Sinai, their impatience led them to idolatry. Study what happens in Exodus 32:1-10.

Even though the people had gotten out of Egypt, Egypt hadn't gotten out of the people. They were so ingrained in a culture that worshiped many idols that they reverted to their former ways. Since they didn't have an idol, they decided to make one. The situation must make you curious though. Where would a bunch of recent slaves get such a bounty of gold to craft such an ornate statue? The account says they used their jewelry (Exod. 32:3-4), but where would these poor people get such lavish accessories? Read Exod. 11:1-3 and 12:33-36 to find out the tragic answer.

How did they get that jewelry?

What a travesty. The people took a gift from God and used it as a replacement for God. God provided that gift. They were wealthy because of his deliverance and not their efforts, and they abandoned him in their prosperity. Growing impatient with God's timing, the people turned to worship the gift instead of the Giver.

What good gifts do you have that run the risk of replacing the Giver?

DAY 2: INVESTIGATE
TWO EVILS

"But my people have changed their glory
for that which does not profit..." (Jer. 2:11).

Jeremiah saw the coming danger. Israel was trending in a dangerous direction. As they walked away from God, they were also walking towards other gods.

Read Jeremiah 2:1-5.

He says the people went after worthless things and became worthless themselves.
What are frivolous things that people pursue in our day?

Read Jeremiah 2:6-13.

The people had forgotten what God had done for them. It led them to do two evils. One was something they abandoned, and the other was something they created. Even if you don't feel artistic, make a simple drawing of the two evils below. It will help you understand them.

EVIL #1   **EVIL #2**
(2:13a)   **(2:13b)**

What major differences do you see of these water supplies?

What are potential cisterns that you have shaped?

COUNT IT AS LOSS

Indeed, I count everything as loss because of the surpassing worth of knowing Christ Jesus my Lord (Phil. 3:8).

God used Paul uniquely to articulate the necessary beliefs and appropriate behaviors of the Christian faith. He had an impressive religious heritage, but it was not what he counted as most important. Each of us must be aware of the dangers of performing religious acts for God instead of pursuing relational connections with God. Read about the change that happened in Paul in Philippians 3:2-6.

Paul could have easily bragged about his religious progress. **What do you have that is commendable in your spiritual history?**

Look at how he described his change in 3:7-11.

Paul went from knowing about the Lord to knowing the Lord, and the difference was paramount! He considered even his manmade religious activities as rubbish compared to knowing Christ finally. Paul could endure the loss of anything because the surpassing worth of knowing Jesus forever anchored him. When was the last time you were in awe of the fact that you get to know Jesus? Take some time in the space below to write a prayer to him. **Thank him for the delight of knowing one so glorious.**

GOD IS THE GREATER JOY

You have put more joy in my heart than they have when
their grain and wine abound (Ps. 4:7).

Plenty of things can provide temporal happiness, but only one can bring eternal joy. David had been through so many difficult times in his life; he knew the power of God's rescuing ability. Whenever he remembered God's activity in his life, he reoriented his joy was to the proper place. Read Psalm 4:1-8 and notice the progression of David's delight.

In times of trouble, David prayed to God for deliverance (4:1-3), committed to obeying God during the process (4:4-5), maintained God as the greater joy (4:6-7), and rested in God until the situation was resolved (4:8). Can you say the same? Fill out the information below to help you process your next steps.

- **What am I praying for God to do?**

- **What disobedience am I tempted to justify?**

- **Is there something providing more joy than God?**

- **Am I trusting in his response and timing?**

David said that God had put more joy in his heart "than they have when their grain and wine abound" (Ps. 4:7). God is the greater joy than any joy this world has to offer. He is better than the most delectable meal or the most satisfying drink. Delighting in God based upon the opportunity is remarkably different than associating with God due to an obligation.

Is God the greatest joy of your life? What other "table" do you continue to frequent?

DON'T BE A DEMAS

Do your best to come to me soon.
(2 Tim. 4:9).

On Paul's many missionary trips, he always took others with him. During these journeys, he was intentional to disciple these associates. Through his travels, you can see those who once served as assistants had been sent to other locations to serve as leaders. In many of his letters, we read different indicators about the status of one of his companions.

One of his partners who is not as famous as some of the others is a man named Demas. He is mentioned only three times in the New Testament. While not much is described about him, what biographical information is available speaks volumes. Read the following passages in their chronological order. Beside each reference, write out any information that Paul gives us about Demas.

- **Colossians 4:14**

- **Philemon 1:23-24**

- **2 Timothy 4:9-10**

2 Timothy is believed to be Paul's final letter before he was martyred. While Paul awaited his execution for following Jesus, during the time of his most profound need for companionship and encouragement, his former friend and co-laborer left him because he loved the world too much. Does Demas' legacy run in your veins? You cannot delightfully prioritize Jesus when you are determinedly pleasuring yourself with the things of this world. **What rival joy of this world must you dethrone in your life?**

DELIGHT REVIEW

To review this week, how do you plan to delight yourself in the LORD more than anything in this world?

Discipleship must be motivated by the wondrous delight of knowing Jesus.

1. What do you currently delight in more than Jesus?

2. What reasonings (good or bad) do you have to grow right now?

3. Would you describe your opportunity to follow Jesus as something that brings you joy? Why or why not?

4. How will you know when you are following Jesus out of delight?

PLAN NOTES

Category #1:

I need to **delight** in Jesus more than

What must be done to see this happen?

CONFRONTING
DISOBEDIENCE

Therefore, since we are surrounded by so great a cloud of witnesses, let us also lay aside every weight, and the sin which clings so closely, and let us run with endurance the race that is set before us (Heb. 12:1).

There is a sin or a few sins that easily entangle you. While we all can struggle with every possible sin imaginable, there are certain sins with which we regularly drift. In Session 3 of Distinctive Discipleship, we are going to narrow down a list of sins to one area which is critical for you to address right now.

CONSIDER

If you had to compile a list of the top 10 sins devastating our culture right now, what sins would you consider as most rampant? Fill out this list as an individual, and then share your list with a small group. Each of you starts by sharing one item. If someone mentions an item on your list, put a star beside it and don't read that one when it is your turn.

1.   6.

2.   7.

3.   8.

4.   9.

5.   10.

As you discussed these sins, your group probably had some recurring items on each other's list. You might have heard some other ideas with which you agree. Look again at this list. Considering these specific sins, some impact you more than others. Some of those sins listed might represent a real struggle for you, and others have never even fazed you in the slightest degree.

If you feel comfortable to do so, draw a target beside 1-3 of those items that either personally causes you to stumble or potentially could cause a threat to your discipleship. **Of which items do you need to pay attention?**

There is a sin or a few sins that cling so closely to you. In this session, we must discover what they are and determine a plan to combat your specific temptation.

STUDY

Turn in your Bible to Hebrews 12. We are going to study a passage that further explains a distinct nature of disobedience. In the Book of Hebrews, the author is on a mission to prove that Jesus is better than anything else you can imagine. In the description of sin, the author's solution to fighting sin is by treasuring Jesus more.

As you read Hebrews 12:1-2, look for the author's description of confronting sin.

What phrases stuck out to you in these verses?

In Heb. 12:1, you notice that the author spoke of a great cloud of witnesses surrounding us. Who are they? The "therefore" at the beginning of the verse helps us understand that the author must have just mentioned these witnesses. In fact, the writer archived 16 biblical figures in Hebrews 11. From Abel to David, the author shows how these distinct individuals all experienced different trials but proved to be faithful through their lives. These people weren't perfect, but they did show progress.

Can you name an area of disobedience for these people mentioned? If you are unsure, use the accompanying verses to discover the answers.

- **Abraham (Gen. 12:10-13)**

- **Moses (Deut. 32:48-52)**

- **Sarah (Gen. 18:9-15)**

- **Rahab (Joshua 2:1)**

- **Jacob (Gen. 27:14-20)**

- **David (2 Sam. 11:2-5, 14-15)**

Even in the Bible's archive of faith heroes, we see each of them with certain challenges and particular propensities towards specific sins. In those descriptions, you might discover unique struggles with which to relate and others that you honestly can't imagine. So why are these wayward figures contained in such a list? While all were sinners (Rom. 3:23), these individuals portrayed a faith in God's promises amid their blatant inconsistencies.

Look at how the author described Moses in Heb. 11:24-26. **How would you summarize Moses' thinking regarding sin?**

Moses is a part of that great cloud of witnesses (Heb. 12:1). Their examples are not perfect track records but progressive faith stories. God brought about hope for many seemingly hopeless cases. Like Moses, many of these individuals ended better than they started. The author of Hebrews wants us to keep their stories in mind as we fight against sin. In these verses, we discover four steps of which we should remember:

1. Learn From Those Before You

2. Lay Aside the Sin That Entangles You

3. Labor Through the Race Before You

4. Look to Jesus Who Can Keep You

DISCUSS

Within your group, answer these following questions:

1. **Learn From Those Before You** - What person from the Bible or in your life fought sin well? What was his or her strategy?

2. **Lay Aside the Sin That Entangles You** - Have you ever noticed that the people in your family can all live in the same environment and yet struggle with different sins? How have you seen that? Why do you think we each get entangled in different ways?

3. **Labor Through the Race Before You** - Why do you think the author indicates that this race fighting against sin must be run with endurance? What does that look like in the life of the believer?

4. **Look to Jesus Who Can Keep You** - Why do you think the author teaches us to look at Jesus rather than the sin? How do we practically do that in our daily walks?

EVALUATE

It is time to get specific. In your Distinctive Discipleship plan, what is the particular sin that you need to confront immediately? **What is currently entangling you and tripping you up as you seek to follow Jesus?**

While it is doubtful that you need a list to remind you of your sins, read the following passages if you need some biblical reminders: 1 Cor. 6:9-10; Gal 5:19-21; Eph. 5:3-6; Rev. 22:15; Prov. 6:16-19.

In developing your plan, you need to address at least one sin but no more than three. If you don't feel comfortable writing it out, use some type of code to indicate what you must address.

	DISOBEDIENCE What is the sin?	DANGER How is it affecting you?	DESIGN How will you fight?
1			
2			
3			

SHARE

While these issues have varying degrees of sensitivity about them, confession is good for us because it brings needed spiritual healing in our lives (James 5:16), it encourages others to do the same (Acts 19:18), it helps us avoid additional sin (James 5:19-20), and it reminds us of our need for forgiveness (1 John 1:9).

If you are willing, would you share an area of disobedience that you need to address?

Would you share the danger of what the disobedience is doing in your life right now? What are the consequences?

As you share, you might find that you are not alone and that others have struggled the same way (1 Cor. 10:13). Do you have any advice for anyone in the group regarding how you have fought a similar fight? Your experience might assist another as he or she develops a personal Distinctive Discipleship plan.

Take some time to pray for another in the group. Depending upon the comfort of the group, each of you prays for the person on your right either audibly or quietly. Pray that the Spirit would work in your lives as you develop plans to combat the disobedience present.

SESSION NOTES

If you are reading the *Distinctive Discipleship* book to accompany this study, read **chapter 6** before coming to the group next time.

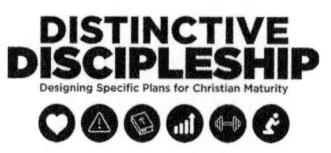

DEAD TO SIN

How can we who died to sin still live in it? (Rom. 6:2).

Theologically speaking, we are dead to sin. Practically speaking, it seems alive and well among us. Thinking through the areas of disobedience that you plan to address, how are we supposed to put those sins to death? Read Romans 6:1-14. As you read, look for phrases that teach you why or how you are to live as if sin is dead to you. Write down those phrases below:

We do not continue to sin so that we can experience grace more (Rom. 6:1). Our identification with Christ's death on the cross means that the sin he paid for should remain dead to us. The world has been crucified to us, and we to the world (Gal. 6:14).

As you read Rom. 6:12-14, Paul provided both things to do and not to do. What are they?

DO THIS: **DON'T DO THIS:**

While you will continue to struggle with sin, you should not surrender to sin. It no longer has dominion over you (Rom. 6:14). Stop obeying its passions.

Pray about your distinct areas of disobedience. Pray that God would give you the strength to confront your sin. Ask God to show you how to use your life to replace unrighteous deeds with righteous opportunities.

DAY 2: INVESTIGATE
THE SPIRIT VS. THE FLESH

...walk by the Spirit, and you will not gratify the desires of the flesh (Gal. 5:16).

In Christ, you are no longer a sinner. You are a saint who sins often. While sin may still be a part of your activity, it is no longer your identity. The battle you experience in confronting disobedience is because your flesh is at war with your spirit.

Read Paul's description in Gal. 5:16-18. **What evidences do you see in your own life that the Spirit is at conflict with your flesh?**

Now read his description of the works of the flesh and the fruit of the Spirit in Gal. 5:19-26.

Based on your preexisting list of 1-3 areas of disobedience you are combatting, how does the fruit of the Spirit go against those temptations? Write down your list of sins on the left, and then write out a characteristic of the fruit of the Spirit that counteracts that tendency.

SINS OF DISOBEDIENCE　　　　　　　**FRUIT OF THE SPIRIT**

Your confrontation of disobedience is not only what you need to stop doing, but it also includes what you need to start doing. Pray and ask God that those particular characteristics of the fruit of the Spirit would be found in you today.

HOW JESUS BEAT TEMPTATION

"It is written, 'Man shall not live by bread alone,
but by every word that comes from the mouth of God'" (Matt. 4:4).

If we want to confront our disobedience, there is no better example to imitate than that of Jesus. Not only did he live his entire live devoid of sin, but he also showed us a powerful strategy in combatting Satan.

Read Matthew 4:1-11.

After Jesus had fasted forty days and nights, he was undoubtedly spiritually prepared, but he was also undeniably physically weak. Satan intentionally came to him at such an opportune moment (Luke 4:13). After no food for almost six weeks, Satan decides to tempt Jesus with bread. What was Jesus' response? He never qualified his desire, but he quoted God's Word. Through three temptations, Jesus quoted three verses. Can you find what verse Jesus was quoting each time? You probably have it in a footnote in your Bible.

Matt. 4:4 -   **Matt. 4:7 -**   **Matt. 4:10 -**

Jesus' victory over temptation was partly due to his rehearsing of God's Word in those moments. As Satan learned his strategy, he even attempted to employ Scripture, but he took it out of context and used it for his own agenda (Matt. 4:6; cf. Ps. 91:11, 12) – an appealing yet hazardous practice you need to avoid.

Thinking through your disobedience list, find 2-3 verses per sin that you will memorize in order to combat temptation. Write them down below. Begin working on the first one and pray that God uses that Word during moments of temptation.

DAY 4: INITIATE

EVICTION DAY

*...that altar with the high place he pulled down and burned,
reducing it to dust (2 Kings 23:15).*

To confront our disobedience, we may need to resort to some drastic measures. We don't send an alcoholic to a bar for rehab. We get them away from the source of temptation as much as possible. For you to find success, you might need to evict some dangerous things in your life.

King Josiah reigned over Judah for 18 years in ignorance concerning God's Law. One day, a servant discovered a copy of Genesis-Deuteronomy and read it before the king. He was overwhelmed. Look what he did in 2 Kings 22:8-20.

Due to his repentant heart, God was not going to make him experience the coming judgment. God was going to keep their enemies at bay until Josiah died, but that wasn't enough for him. Even though God spared him from punishment, Josiah wanted to rid himself and his land of sin's pollution. With the promise of his security, look at the drastic measures he took in 2 Kings 23:1-20.

It wasn't enough that King Josiah was forgiven of sin; he wanted to remove the temptation. Through sweeping reforms and drastic measures, he reduced the possibility of further idolatry.

Considering your disobedience list, what drastic measures do you need to take? Is there anything or anyone in your life that will complicate your progress?

Write those stumbling blocks down and ask God to show you what you need to evict.

FIGHT TO THE DEATH

...if by the Spirit you put to death the deeds of the body, you will live (Rom. 8:13).

Your battle plan is useless if you never implement it. To confront your disobedience, you must engage in the battle and to fight to the death. In this week's devotions, we have learned about the nature of sin, the fruit of the Spirit, the need to memorize Scripture, and the task of evicting opportunities for sin. As we wrap up this week, make sure you have a plan in place.

Read Romans 8:12-14.

According to Paul, something has to die – you or your flesh. You put to death the deeds of the flesh by the power of the Spirit. The Spirit emboldens you to challenge, encourages ways to combat, and equips you with tools to resist, so that you can wage war against the sin that so easily entangles you. By putting up a fight, you are engaging in battle and pushing back the enemy lines.

Think about your top area of disobedience you plan to combat. You are not the only person struggling with that issue (1 Cor. 10:13). What if someone that you care deeply about approached you with the same area of disobedience? What if you saw how much it was affecting his or her life? **What decisive plan would you give him or her? Have you implemented a similar strategy for your own life?**

Your battle against temptation will benefit you, but your battle tactics might also save another. Pray as you begin to implement your plan that you can put these deeds of the flesh to death.

DISOBEDIENCE REVIEW

To recap this week, how do you plan to confront disobedience in your Distinctive Discipleship plan?

Discipleship must warn against disobedience in any sinful leanings specific to the person.

1. What major sins do you plan to address?

2. What next steps do you plan to take?

3. What has your mentor or partner instructed you to consider?

4. Is there any component of the plan of which you are still unsure? If you are missing some piece needed to start, write down a reminder here so you can address it once you complete the plan.

PLAN NOTES

Category #2:

My **disobedience** that must be addressed is

What are my necessary steps?

SESSION 4

STRENGTHENING DOCTRINE

Do your best to present yourself to God as one approved, a worker who has no need to be ashamed, rightly handling the word of truth (2 Tim. 2:15).

Are you confident in the fundamentals of your faith? Maybe the better question is, do you believe what you believe? As a follower of Jesus, you have a set of doctrinal beliefs that come along with the territory. Biblical Christianity is blatant on topics in which the culture will struggle to accept. In Session 4 of Distinctive Discipleship, we are going to hone in on one doctrinal concept that you need to study next.

CONSIDER

Wayne Grudem is a Christian professor and author. Many seminary professors utilize his *Systematic Theology* textbook in many settings. At 1291 pages, it is a comprehensive volume. Due to its size, he also summarized the content into a 528-page book entitled *Bible Doctrine*. If that content is still too inaccessible, he developed a 159-page condensed form in a book called *Christian Beliefs*. While all three books cover similar topics, they vary in the degree of the specific content.

If you had to choose one of those textbooks to describe your current understanding of biblical doctrine, which one would you use to describe yourself? Using the scale underneath the icons below, place an "X" where you are right now and place a circle where you think you should be at this stage in your walk.

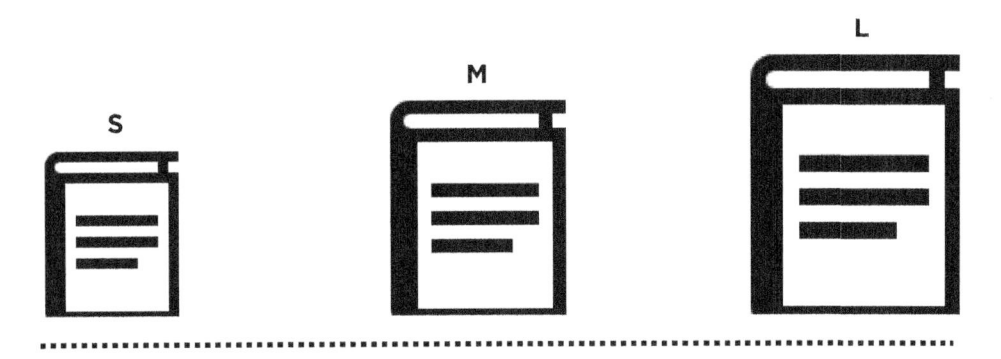

In the group, share the textbook designations you gave yourself and why. **What are the positive reasons for why you are where you are? Why would you say that you aren't further along by this point in your life? Write your answers below before sharing with the group.**

Even if you feel that you should have more knowledge than you do right now, you do have some. In reality, if you rated yourself on the low end of that scale, you know more Bible than someone in your life. Even if your theology is on the small textbook side, those truths would be incredibly beneficial to someone in the early stages of faith development. What biblical knowledge you take for granted might be life changing for someone spiritually behind you. Don't wait till you are an expert before you share what you have at this moment.

What is something you know from the Bible that you could share with another?

While guilt may attempt to discourage your current doctrinal understanding, discipleship provides hope for the needed path of doctrinal clarity. A more beneficial use of your time is to consider what you can learn now rather than regret what you haven't learned yet.

STUDY

Open your Bible to 2 Timothy 2. The Apostle Paul wrote this letter to his disciple, Timothy. Paul invested everything he had into Timothy for ministry multiplication. Most likely Paul's last letter, 2 Timothy records his concern for Timothy's doctrine in trying times. We would be wise to heed his advice.

Have someone in the group read 2 Timothy 2:14-19 aloud. Take a brief pause at the end of each verse to notate some reflections. As you follow along, write down words from the passage in the columns below. **What are the keywords that Paul uses to describe solid doctrine and swerving beliefs?**

SOLID DOCTRINE   **SWERVING BELIEFS**

As a group, share the words you noticed that described these two designations.

While you may not know much about Hymenaeus and Philetus (2 Tim. 2:17), you know enough to understand them just by studying these verses. **How does Paul describe these two?**

How do you see contemporary trends going in the same direction as these two individuals?

Most people don't spin from the truth – they swerve from the truth. Paul taught Timothy the nature of moving from biblical doctrine. It is more often a gradual turning rather than an about-face (2 Tim. 2:18).

For all the theological controversies around Timothy, Paul reminded him of the firm foundation that God's truth brings (2 Tim. 2:19). In any changing culture, we are lured into a way of thinking that says God needs to get up to speed with our thinking. If God's truth is perfect, it is also timeless. Doctrines given by God will never require our revision. Read these words archived by the Apostle Peter:

> *Since you have been born again, not of perishable seed but of imperishable, through the living and abiding word of God; for "All flesh is like grass, and all its glory like the flower of grass. The grass withers, and the flower falls, but the word of the Lord remains forever" (1 Pet. 1:23-25).*

Our salvation comes through not an ancient book but the living and abiding word of God! As men and women of flesh, we are like the grass that withers and dies. Flowery ideas will spring up through the years, but they waste away into brittle stems within a mere season. Every new and updated concept has a limited shelf life, but God's Word remains forever.

Even within Peter's description is a subtle yet mesmerizing detail about God's truth. He quotes from the prophet Isaiah at the end of his words (Isa. 40:7-8). Peter was born about 700 years after Isaiah penned those words, and yet they still maintained truthful vibrancy because God's Word never fades. If it endured to Peter's life, is it still powerful enough to persevere unto our day?

DISCUSS

What does it mean to be approved by God when it comes to handling Scripture (2 Tim. 2:15)?

What type of understanding do you think would please God? Regardless of what size theology textbook's information is in your head, you have some level of biblical knowledge. Paul instructed Timothy to do his best so that he would not be ashamed. Regarding doctrine, where are you confident, and where would you be embarrassed?

Let's do a simple biblical diagnostic test.

1. **Go to your Bible's table of contents. With which Old Testament book are you the most familiar?**

2. **Which Old Testament book have you had the least exposure?**

3. **What is your most read New Testament book?**

4. **Which New Testament book have you forgotten or ignored?**

5. **Is there a type of doctrinal debate that you seek to avoid because of controversy or confusion?**

After answering these questions on your own, share your answers with the group.

What did you notice about the group's answers?

EVALUATE

Paul instructed Timothy to do his personal best in studying doctrine (2 Tim. 2:15). He didn't tell him to do the best of Paul his mentor, Titus his peer, Eunice his mother, or Lois his grandmother. Paul wanted Timothy to bring his absolute best he could do to the task of learning biblical doctrine.

What is the danger in comparing our current biblical comprehension to someone else? In the space below, write down the name or the initials of someone who knows the Bible less than you and someone who knows it more than you. Besides those names, then provide reasons for that gap given their situations.

BIBLE APPRENTICE   **BIBLE SCHOLAR**

NAME:

REASONING:

As you think through the different reasonings for everyone's place, you may have noticed that consistent exposure was probably more critical than just natural mental faculties. You can learn the Bible if you decide to study the Bible. Our biblical ignorance is more of a priority problem than an ability problem.

In Col. 1:28, Paul said that we need to teach everyone with all wisdom. So what part of God's wisdom do you need to commit to studying next? It might be a book of the Bible, or it could be that doctrinal stance of which you are unsure. While we all have numerous issues on which we could improve, now is the time to select one doctrinal weakness that you plan to strengthen.

In your selection, don't select a curious topic but choose a critical issue. Decide to investigate a doctrine that is crucial for your faith formation.

Brainstorm in the section below a few topics that you could commit to studying. What are some possibilities? After writing down some options, rank them with a number beside each one. Put a star by the most critical doctrinal issue that you need to address.

SHARE

In your group, share the top doctrinal issue that you desire to study in the coming months. After one person shares, allow time for the group to offer feedback or potential resources to help in the individual's plan.

Write down any ideas given to you from the group as you formalize your Distinctive Discipleship plan.

As you concluded this session, have someone read Psalm 119:17-24 and have someone pray those verses over the group.

SESSION NOTES

If you are reading the **Distinctive Discipleship** book to accompany this study, read **chapter 7** before coming to the group next time.

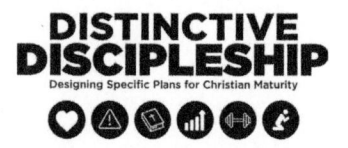

SUPPLY WHAT IS LACKING

...and we pray most earnestly night and day that we may see you face to face and supply what is lacking in your faith (1 Thess. 3:10).

Paul traveled to Thessalonica and experienced fruitful ministry very quickly. He saw such success (Acts 17:4) that it caused great hostility from certain locals and forced Paul and his missionary companions to leave the city prematurely (Acts 17:9-10). Since Paul was unable to invest a sufficient amount of time teaching these new believers and hindered from returning (1 Thess. 2:18), he sent Timothy to visit them (1 Thess. 3:1-2) and wrote the letter we know as 1 Thessalonians.

Read Paul's reaction to Timothy's report from his visit in 1 Thess. 3:6-10.

Per Timothy's visit, this young church was doing well. Paul was encouraged by their faith, love, and kindness. For all the good that Timothy saw, he must have seen something else that sincerely burdened Paul. He wanted to visit again in order to supply what was lacking in their faith (1 Thess. 3:10). Without enough time to disciple these new believers in the fundamental areas of faith, they lacked some doctrinal clarity. If you look at the following subheadings in the book, you might notice what some of their doctrinal needs were. **What do the subheadings in chapters 3-4 indicate about their weak areas? What were they?**

If Paul was to hear a report on your doctrinal understanding, what would he say? What topics would he find necessary to teach you?

CONDONING BAD DOCTRINE

"But I have a few things against you: you have some there
who hold the teaching of Balaam..." (Rev. 2:14).

In the beginning chapters of the Book of Revelation, Jesus serves as a church consultant to seven churches throughout the Asian region. Among each congregation, he gives specific commendations and other condemnations. The church at Ephesus was victorious in resisting and exposing false teachers, but the church at Pergamum did not have the same propensity.

Notice Jesus' rebuke of the people as you read Rev. 2:12-17.

The city was apparently so vile that Jesus would call it the location of Satan's throne (Rev. 2:13). These believers were suffering from persecution, and even one member was martyred for his faith (Rev. 2:13). While Jesus praised them for their faithful endurance through trials, he criticized them for their fuzzy commitment to truth. While you may not know all of the specifics regarding the two heretical groups mentioned (Rev. 2:14-15), you do know enough from the description that unbiblical beliefs lead to ungodly behavior.

What type of faulty doctrine are believers tempted to condone today?

What was Jesus' solution for the dangerous tendency to compromise? He mentioned a weapon that he would use to combat such an assault (Rev. 2:12, 16). What exactly does he imply by such a weapon (if unsure, read Heb. 4:12)? **How will picking up this weapon help you?**

GROW IN GRACE & KNOWLEDGE

But grow in the grace and knowledge of our Lord and Savior Jesus Christ
(2 Pet. 3:18).

Peter knew all too well the danger of attempting to alter God's truth. He had once resisted accepting the reality of who Jesus was for a version he preferred more (Matt. 16:21-23). Peter's thoughts were on man more than God. Jesus staunchly rebuked him for such unthinkable rebellion.

Later in his life, Peter understood the need to embrace God's truth as well as avoid man's opinion. Read his warning to other believers in 2 Pet. 3:14-18.

Within the final words of his letter, Peter emphasized the connection between behavior and belief. He showed the sacred awareness of Paul's writings when he remarkably equated his letters as Scripture (2 Pet. 3:16). As he warned these believers not to be carried away with theological errors, he revealed the protection against such a tragedy – "grow in the grace and knowledge of our Lord and Savior Jesus Christ" (2 Pet. 3:18). How are we to avoid drifting towards dangerous heresy? Continue to strengthen biblical clarity.

Can you think of a time in your life when you loved the Word of God more than you do right now? **If so, write down when that was and why you think it was that way.**

Hopefully, you realized some necessary elements that made the difference during that time. **How will you pray for God to reignite that passion again?**

KEEP A CLOSE WATCH

Keep a close watch on yourself and on the teaching. Persist in this,
for by so doing you will save both yourself and your hearers (1 Tim. 4:16).

In Paul's commitment to disciple Timothy, he seemed to indicate that he believed in his disciple more than the disciple believed in himself. With Paul's encouragement to fan the flame (2 Tim. 1:6), records of commending him to other people (Phil. 2:20), and exhorting not to sell himself short due to age or experience (1 Tim. 4:12), he saw the great potential in Timothy's life. Read Paul's instructions to him in 1 Tim. 4:11-16.

What words stick out to you in this passage regarding doctrine?

Paul expected Timothy to teach. He didn't have to be ashamed about his age because the doctrinal truths he would proclaim were eternal. Paul encouraged public and private devotion to the Scriptures. He wanted Timothy to do more than interact with God's Word; he wanted him to immerse himself in its truth (1 Tim. 4:15).

One shocking warning is that his teaching not only affected his own soul but those who listened to him as well. Have you ever realized that if you have a poor understanding of doctrine, those who look up to you will probably inherit that level of comprehension as well? Below, list names of those who will be impacted by your knowledge of Scripture. No matter how much you know, you are a standard to someone else. Pray that God would use you to make a positive impact on them.

DAY 5: IMPLEMENT

THE SOLUTION FOR ITCHING EARS

For the time is coming when people will not endure sound teaching,
but having itching ears they will accumulate for themselves teachers
to suit their own passions (2 Tim. 4:3).

Instead of listening to what we need to hear, we tend to gravitate towards people who tell us what we want to hear. Paul prepared Timothy that people would drift away from biblical teaching and align with teachers who placed approval stamps upon unbiblical beliefs and behaviors. Read the description of these people in 2 Tim. 3:14-4:5.

Timothy was exposed to Scripture at an early age from his mother and grandmother (2 Tim. 3:14-15; cf. 1:5). **Who are the teachers that exposed you to biblical teaching during your spiritual journey?**

While Timothy started in the truth, Paul wanted to ensure that he also ended in the truth. The truths contained in the Bible are profitable for teaching (what is right), reproof (what is wrong), correction (how to make it right), and training (how to keep it right) [2 Tim. 3:16]. Understanding that the times would continue to reveal more people drifting away from biblical teaching, Paul encouraged Timothy to study the truth from God's perspective rather than the opinions deriving from his own passions (2 Tim. 4:3).

Is there a dangerous doctrinal area in your mind? What areas are you inwardly questioning regarding a loophole in Scripture? **Write those down and ensure they are on your doctrinal list to study.**

SESSION 4

DOCTRINE REVIEW

To recap this week, how do you plan to strengthen doctrine in your Distinctive Discipleship plan?

Discipleship must wisely equip the follower to possess increasingly competent biblical doctrine.

1. What specific doctrines do you plan to strengthen?

2. What next steps do you plan to take in your study?

3. What has your mentor or partner instructed you to consider?

4. What resources will you need to identify to prepare for intentional study?

PLAN NOTES

Category #3:

The pivotal **doctrine** for me to study is

What is my action plan?

SESSION 5
CLARIFYING
DEVELOPMENT

When I was a child, I spoke like a child, I thought like a child, I reasoned like a child. When I became a man, I gave up childish ways (1 Cor. 13:11).

In what ways do you need development? It all depends upon what you have been given and where you have been placed. As particularly gifted and positioned disciples, we each should pursue the needed maturity to do what God has called us to accomplish. In Session 5, we will focus on clarifying your personal development as part of your Distinctive Discipleship plan. The development piece comes from Paul's charge that "we may present everyone mature in Christ" (Col. 1:28). You could envision a mentor presenting a disciple to God, saying, "I did everything I could to help this individual develop in distinct ways." This category is unique from the others in that it seeks to develop you in tangible ways for ministry growth.

CONSIDER

There's a difference in working on something because you are supposed to learn it versus you are desperate to know it. Each of us knows the stark contrast between being eager and being resistant. In the list below, write down some pieces of knowledge or skill that you had to learn. Beside each item, list a reason for why you felt negative or positive towards that training.

EAGER	WHY?	RESISTANT	WHY?

In your group, share an item from both sides of your list and the reason you gave for each one.

Within that discussion, you probably realized that the reason you resented distinct development processes in your life is that you saw no value in training.

For those opportunities, you saw them most likely as necessary or beneficial. We don't mind working hard for something that we value highly.

- Couples address their marriage due to desire or disagreements.

- Parents invest in their children due to compassion or concern.

- Training for work is sought for promotion or protection.

- Exercise is employed when there is a risk or a reward.

The list could go on further, but we seem to find motivation for development when we either feel a potential risk or an exciting prospect. In this session, we are going to discover an area in your life that you need to develop. Let's find it together.

STUDY

Turn in your Bible to Exodus 18. The context for this passage follows Moses overseeing the Israelites after God rescued them from slavery. God showed his power through the ten plagues and the parting sea, and these people were on the way to the Promised Land. Along the path, they experienced issues for which Moses had to govern. One day, Moses' father-in-law, Jethro, came to visit him. Look what happened in Exodus 18:1-12. As you read, watch for the change that transpired in Jethro.

What happened to Jethro as a result of Moses' testimony (18:10-12)?

Jethro was leaving this moment a different man due to the work of God among Moses. **Why do you think our personal stories of deliverance can be so effective in sharing with non-believers?**

After this event, Jethro wanted to follow Moses to work to see what his son-in-law did all day. What he saw was incredibly revealing. Read his discovery and response in Exodus 18:13-27.

What did Jethro notice about Moses?

What kind of cases do you think Moses had to address?

How did Jethro encourage Moses to change?

Even though Jethro was in the early stages of faith development, he was still a wise, older man. All wisdom is God's wisdom, and Jethro had learned some of it through his life. He looked at this growing leader and imparted some practical advice so that Moses could do what he did but do it better. While this story is often rightfully taught on the effectiveness of delegation, don't miss out on what happens after Exodus 18. In Exodus 19, Moses scaled Mt. Sinai, and the LORD came down to meet with him there (Exod. 19:18-20). In Exodus 20, God gave Moses the 10 Commandments that forever altered the trajectory of an international standard of morality.

Could Moses have discovered the margin to meet with God if he was continuing to address upset travelers in dispute with one another? Jethro's practical tip related to improving Moses' vocation opened the door to experience God's revelation. Moses met God on Sinai because Jethro equipped him to do so at Rephidim.

DISCUSS

In the last chapter of the Old Testament, Malachi wrote: "Remember the law of my servant Moses, the statutes and rules that I commanded him at Horeb for all Israel" (Mal. 4:4). From the initial giving of the Law in Exodus 20 to the last chapter in the Old Testament in Malachi 4, the Law was pivotal to the direction of the people. It even formulated Jesus' preaching in Matthew 5.

While God can use any means necessary to accomplish his purposes, he saw fit that our exposure to the Law happened due to the wisdom of an older man who gave practical advice on how to clear a calendar and improve a process. The example of Jethro honestly provides an excellent method for intentional discipleship within the context of relationships.

Jethro instructed Moses in a way that is easy to imitate and replicate. If you feel overwhelmed at discipling another, consider the practical steps he portrayed.

1. **Proximity** (Exod. 18:1-12): Find a potential disciple from within your existing relationships.

2. **Assessment** (Exod. 18:13-14a): Evaluate the spiritual health and ministry success of the individual.

3. **Initiation** (Exod. 18:14b-16): Take the initiative to help someone with great potential.

4. **Challenge** (Exod. 18:17): Identify key areas that the person needs to address.

5. **Instruction** (Exod. 18:18-23): Provide reasonable and practical wisdom for the person.

6. **Application** (Exod. 18:24-27): Oversee the person during implementation until it is passed on to another.

Out of those six stages, which one do you think is the most intimidating, and why?

Even though Jethro wasn't that spiritually mature, he did have something very tangible with which to help Moses. **What are common inadequacies to why you feel as if you can't disciple someone else?**

Jethro provided practical help to Moses that reaped spiritual rewards. Moses' need was unique to his situation. He didn't need help in delegation before this time in his life, but God brought him support at a specific time. As we begin to narrow your scope, let's think through ways that many people need to be developed. These might be practical areas, but they are related to the overall maturity of the individual (Col. 1:28).

What are the practical ways that people need training in the following categories?

- **Successful Vocation**:

- **Healthy Marriage**:

- **Intentional Parenting**:

- **Church Involvement**:

- **Personal Finances**:

- **Life Skills**:

EVALUATE

As a group, you shared many ideas of which someone might need to be developed. Which are the ones most pertinent to you right now? On the list above, circle 3-5 that you would benefit from a little more intentionality.

While you might see many real needs, we need to narrow down these items to a realistic priority list. As you consider those above, you might also need to include some additional ones. These aren't issues of iniquity as much as they are areas for improvement. Let's narrow the focus even more and get as specific as possible.

- **Family**: What is the most helpful skill you need with your family right now?

- **Church**: As you serve in the ministry of your church, what spiritual gift or practice of yours could you further develop?

- **Personal**: As you consider loving God with all your strength, is there an area in your life that you need to address?

As you look at those three areas, you must be realistic in deciding which ones to address at this point in your life. **Where is the most dangerous risk or the most significant prospect?**

SHARE

In your group, share an item that you desire to develop in your Distinctive Discipleship plan. As you share your selection, allow other people in the group to give you ideas or resources that might help. Write down those notes beside your list above.

As a group, talk through how you will get to work on these. What is the next step? Pray for one another as you embark on fleshing out your plan for development.

SESSION NOTES

If you are reading the **Distinctive Discipleship** book to accompany this study, read **chapter 8** before coming to the group next time.

FEARFULLY & WONDERFULLY

I praise you, for I am fearfully and wonderfully made.
Wonderful are your works; my soul knows it very well (Ps. 139:14).

You are unique. God didn't use a template to form you. Your Creator designed every part of your good desires and every one of your noble opportunities. Read Psalm 139:1-18 to see his intentionality. As you read, make a note of words or phrases that speak to the uniqueness of how God created you.

What verses or phrases stuck out to you and why? Write at least three discoveries below.

1.

2.

3.

Have you ever struggled to embrace how God made you? Have you wondered why you are like this and not like that? **When we cast doubt on our distinct design, what are we ultimately saying to God?**

God doesn't make mistakes. To figure out how you need to be developed, you first need to understand how you were designed. What is unique about you? This step might seem awkward, but it is crucial. All of God's works are wonderful, and that includes you (Ps. 139:14)! **What are the noteworthy characteristics and opportunities that God has given specifically to you?**

DAY 2: INVESTIGATE

GOD'S WORKMANSHIP

For we are his workmanship, created in Christ Jesus for good works,
which God prepared beforehand, that we should walk in them (Eph. 2:10).

Not only were you created by someone, but you were created for something. To understand your purpose, you must pursue the one who created you in the first place. God designed you distinct, and that is why your discipleship must be distinct as well.

Read Ephesians 2:8-10 and investigate the nature between our salvation and our designation.

How many good works did God require you to prove before he saved you?

What type of good works should we produce now that God has saved us?

We were not saved by good works, but we were saved for good works. God actually prepared opportunities for these efforts to be utilized. Since each creation is unique, that implies that each opportunity is distinct. God has designed you to produce good works that not every other believer is expected to provide.

For what type of good works do you believe God has designed you?

YOUR APPOINTMENT

"Before I formed you in the womb I knew you, and before you were born
I consecrated you; I appointed you a prophet to the nations" (Jer. 1:5).

Jeremiah served as a prophet during a difficult time in Judah's history. Oftentimes, he talked about quitting because his ministry was so challenging (Jer. 20:9). In the opening pages of his book, he revealed why he would endure to the end even when he often felt like giving up.

Read his description in Jeremiah 1:4-10.

We often think that it is only our experiences and education that prepares us. Too regularly do we assume that our networks solely provide us the opportunities given to us. While much of that is true, we must realize the importance of God's appointment over our lives. Others have taught us that it's not what you know, but who you know that will define our lives. If that is true, we must take to heart that we know God, and he knows us.

Not only does he know us, but he designed us for specific purposes. Before Jeremiah ever took a breath, God appointed the purpose of his breathing. He appointed Jeremiah, and he has appointed every single one of us to particular callings. God appoints people to be intentional fathers and mothers, gifted preachers and teachers, and Kingdom-minded blue-collar workers and white-collar workers.

To what roles do you believe God has appointed you? Write down some of them below and pray that God shows you further how to develop those roles.

TIMOTHY OR TITUS?

So the churches were strengthened in the faith,
and they increased in numbers daily (Acts 16:5).

Paul discipled many people during his life. In his letters to Timothy and Titus, we hear his heart towards two specific young men dear to his heart who were serving in the ministry. While his investment into both of them is noteworthy, he did not treat both of them the same. In fact, he required different acts of commitment from each one depending upon their unique context. Read the following passages and make notes regarding their specific assignments.

TIMOTHY [ACTS 16:1-5]

TITUS [GAL. 2:1-5]

You have to wonder if Timothy ever knew about the "unfair" exception for Titus. Both were living as adult men, serving as pastors, and coming from Greek fathers, yet Paul required circumcision from Timothy and not Titus. Why the differentiation? It all came down to context. Titus was ministering to Greeks, and Timothy was ministering to Jews. In a culture aware of who had performed important rituals, Timothy would have never had an opportunity to minister in that city if he had forsaken circumcision. If Titus had been circumcised, it would have wrongly portrayed a work as necessary for salvation. Due to each one's context, Paul required something unique in their development.

As peculiar as an example as this scenario is, it shows the importance of context determining development. **What settings make your own needs for discipleship unique from another's?**

FINISHING WHAT HE STARTS

And I am sure of this, that he who began a good work in you
will bring it to completion at the day of Jesus Christ (Phil. 1:6).

In the areas of your spiritual development, you might often feel as if the work will never be complete. As soon as you take one step forward, it almost seems as if you take a few steps backward. If your growth was solely left up to you, the task might never reach a satisfying conclusion, but God always finishes what he starts.

Read Paul's description of such a work in Philippians 1:3-11.

How would you describe your first days as a believer?

Considering Phil. 1:6, how would you describe your future days as a believer?

God has promised that he will finish what he started in you. You will gradually show more progress on this earth (1:9-10) and experience perfection once in heaven (1:10-11). You will experience the long-term solution once you see Jesus. **What short-term victories are you hoping will happen in your life through this process of your unique development?**

DEVELOPMENT REVIEW

To review this week, how do you plan to clarify your process of development in your Distinctive Discipleship plan?

Discipleship must address areas of calling with the intention to bring about ministry development.

1. What major area or areas do you plan on developing?

2. If further developed, how will these areas bring God glory?

3. How will these changes in your life help other people?

4. What type of help will you need to get going? What are some elements you know you will need?

PLAN NOTES

Category #4:

I need **development** in learning how to

What is the plan going forward?

INITIATING
DISCIPLINE

Every athlete exercises self-control in all things. They do it to receive a perishable wreath, but we an imperishable (1 Cor. 9:25).

Paul described his work in discipleship as something for which he toiled (Col. 1:29). If that sounds like work to you, it is because spiritual disciplines require consistent, diligent effort on your part. In Session 6 of Distinctive Discipleship, you are going to select the most vital spiritual discipline to strengthen at this time in your life. You will determine which one is best for your soul's health and get to work on it this very day. This discipline will begin to train the habits necessary for your discipleship.

CONSIDER

Practice doesn't make perfect, but it does make progress. You can look around you and notice people who are extremely disciplined for a variety of reasons to improve in certain key areas. What are some specific purposes for which people discipline themselves and why? In your group, give a list of popular disciplined activities with the accompanying hopeful payoffs for each one.

DISCIPLINED ACTIVITY   **HOPEFUL PAYOFF**

Some people give their lives to these disciplines. It is what wakes them up in the morning and keeps them occupied at night. **While many positive benefits potentially exist for the items on your list, what are some of the frustrating or frivolous realities about some of those disciplines?**

Many of the benefits associated with people's most-prized disciplines are unfortunately short-lived. When it comes to spiritual disciplines, these activities do more than improve your life; they develop your soul.

STUDY

As Paul discipled others, he understood the need for disciplining oneself. He encouraged his disciple, Timothy, to train himself for the purpose of godliness (1 Tim 4:7). "For while bodily training is of some value, godliness is of value in every way, as it holds promise for the present life and also for the life to come" (1 Tim 4:8).

The Corinthian church lived in a city obsessed with physical discipline. They loved athletic competitions displaying their physical prowess. What Paul noticed in them was a willingness to discipline their bodies while neglecting to discipline their souls. Read his instruction to this church in 1 Corinthians 9:24-27.

How is spiritual growth similar to athletic preparations and competitions?

How does an athlete exhibit self-control in all things (9:25)?

What should that example look like in the life of the disciple?

These athletes competed for the glory of a perishable wreath (9:25). While it looked beautiful arrayed upon the victor's head on the podium, within days the foliage withered into frail and unbecoming stems. **How does that relate to worldly disciplines?**

How can spiritual disciplines receive imperishable wreaths in contrast?

Not only did Paul teach on the need for spiritual disciplines, but he also practiced it. While he had reason to have confidence in his flesh for previous religious efforts (Phil. 3:4-6), he never wanted to become stagnate. He kept growing. Many of the biblical figures portrayed an example of how to work out those spiritual muscles. Oftentimes, the disciplines practiced in private reaped the benefits in public.

Look up these following passages and fill out the chart together regarding these biblical examples. After reading each section, write out the name of the individual, the discipline you see employed, and any descriptions that speak of how they used these disciplines.

	NAME	DISCIPLINE	DESCRIPTIONS
Ezra 7:10			
Esther 4:15-16			
Daniel 6:10			
Luke 2:36-38			
Matthew 4:4			

DISCUSS

We have seen biblical examples of those who practiced spiritual disciplines, but you have probably seen some personal cases as well. Who in your life exemplified prioritizing these habits? Write down the name and describe why you thought of him and her. **Share with the group the story of the disciplined person who impacted you.**

What are the main reasons we struggle prioritizing spiritual disciplines in our lives?

As your group compiled the list above, which one is your most nagging hindrance? Circle it above and share it with the group.

Oftentimes, people struggle with maintaining a positive motive for initiating spiritual disciplines. If you are developing a spiritual discipline out of guilt, your effort will be short-lived. If anything other than godliness is your purpose for spiritual disciplines (1 Tim. 4:7), you will lose momentum. Spiritual disciplines are not engaged to earn God's love, increase his favor for you, or to help him by supplying something he is lacking. God doesn't need you to spend time with him. If you don't spend time with God, he's not the one missing out – you are.

Spiritual disciplines are not meant to make you more liked by Jesus but to make you more like Jesus. These disciplines are dedicated activities that hopefully turn into joyful habits. The more you commit to starting them, the more you will feel drawn towards continuing them.

Have you ever tried to prioritize a spiritual discipline and eventually quit? What was it, and why did you stop doing it?

Let's make a list of potential spiritual disciplines for you to initiate. **What are regular activities to which you commit that would help grow your spiritual health?**

EVALUATE

As your group compiled the list, you now need to narrow your focus. What will be the next spiritual discipline that you will focus on for continual spiritual growth?

In the list above, designate three items based on which one relates best to the given category.

1. **Draw a circle around the discipline with which you have had the most success.**

2. **Draw a rectangle around the discipline with which you are the most deficient.**

3. **Draw a star beside the discipline that you feel most critical for your growth at this time.**

This Distinctive Discipleship plan is designed as a guide rather than a checklist. The intention is to allow you freedom in choosing what is prioritized in each category. This warning will be unique to this entire process, but if you aren't reading the Bible regularly, you need to make that the discipline that you focus upon next. No discipline is more important than regular Bible study because it encourages every other worthwhile spiritual pursuit. If you feel like you are in a healthy place with that discipline, go to another, but do not neglect this one.

What will be the next spiritual discipline you begin to strengthen?

What process will you use? What resources will you need?

SHARE

Within your group, share which discipline you have selected. Ask for advice or wisdom from anyone in the group who has seen success in that area. Some of your best help will come from those around you. Write those tips down in the section above.

Take some time to pray over one another. Get specific in your prayers that these actions of resolve will become habits of desire.

SESSION NOTES

If you are reading the **Distinctive Discipleship** book to accompany this study, read **chapter 9** before coming to the group next time.

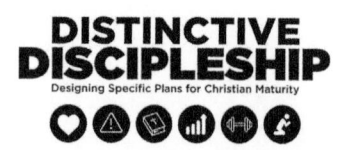

DAY 1: IDENTIFY

DAY & NIGHT

"This Book of the Law shall not depart from your mouth,
but you shall mediate on it day and night" (Josh. 1:8).

If you have ever felt the pressure of stepping into giant shoes of an impressive leader before you, can you imagine what Joshua must have felt taking the lead for God's people after Moses died? The man who confronted Pharaoh, held the staff up for the parting of the Red Sea, and received the Ten Commandments written by Almighty God was dead, and Joshua had to step into command. What would be his comfort?

God provided needed instruction into Joshua's life as his leadership began. Read what God told him in Joshua 1:1-9.

What did God tell Joshua three times within this passage?

Why was that a necessary repeated reminder for Joshua?

How does the description of God's instruction for Joshua's commitment differ from how we often view spiritual disciplines (1:8)?

While meditating on Scripture is the discipline that is highlighted in this passage, the concept is the same for any emphasis you select. You need more than occasional exposure; you need consistent meditation. **What do you think will be a healthy rhythm of the discipline you selected?**

WISDOM & STATURE

And Jesus increased in wisdom and stature and in favor with God and man
(Luke 2:52).

God often provides examples for us to follow. He does things not because they are necessary for him, but because he knows they will be essential for us. When God rested on the seventh day of Creation (Gen. 2:2-3), he was not exhausted (Isa. 40:28) but knew that we would be. He rested as an example so that we would follow behind him.

Before Jesus selected his twelve disciples, he spent an entire night in prayer (Luke 6:12). Jesus was not unsure of who he would chose, but he gave an example for us of a wise practice before a major decision. Much of Jesus' actions were meant to serve as a guide for ours.

Even when Jesus was twelve years old, he was teaching us. Read what he did in Luke 2:41-52.

This account of Jesus is the only one we have between the ages of two and thirty. While Luke reports of a single occurrence, Jesus displayed a beautiful framework. **What do you notice about Jesus in this passage?**

Jesus' commitment to study in religious gatherings guides us to employ discipline in our own lives. If Jesus thought that such dedication was important for his own life, how desperate should we be? **If you want to grow in wisdom and stature, how dedicated should you be to the discipline you have chosen?**

BE A BEREAN

...they received the word with all eagerness,
examining the Scriptures daily to see if these things were so (Acts 17:11).

While the Scriptures are full of expansive descriptions of spiritual mentors, it also contains numerous examples with minimal information yet powerful impact. One such group of people are the Bereans. While Luke doesn't record much about them, what he did write speaks a lot.

Read the description of the Bereans in Acts 17:10-15.

While persecution seemed to follow Paul and his companions wherever they went, they also experienced fruitful ministry. Even among the religious agitators attempting to slow the ministry down (Acts 17:13), a group showed what can happen in a city when a few followers get disciplined (Acts 17:12). The report of the Bereans should make us want to be labeled one as well.

Using the description provided, how should we imitate these Bereans? In Acts 17:11, we see some keywords that we should implement towards our efforts at discipline. How should these words guide your process?

- **Eager**

- **Examine**

- **Daily**

No matter which discipline you have chosen, be like a Berean. Be earnest in your efforts, diligent with your process, and keep your attempts regular by maintaining daily exposure.

SET YOUR HEART

For Ezra had set his heart to study the Law of the LORD,
and to do it and to teach his statutes and rules in Israel (Ezra 7:10).

Ezra was part of the team God used in re-establishing Israel's worship once the remnant returned. After being exiled due to their idolatry, these leaders wanted to make sure they did things right once back in the land. Once they rebuilt the temple, God used Ezra to ensure what happened in the temple was biblical.

Read how his personal discipline impacted corporate worship in Ezra 7:1-10.

God had prepared Ezra, but Ezra wasn't complete. If he wanted to ensure Israel stayed biblical, he had to know the biblical content intimately. In this description, Ezra gives an excellent guide for us to initiate as we work out any spiritual discipline. Ezra made a decision, initiated a habit, committed to application, and then taught others how to do the same (Ezra 7:10). His example is simple to initiate in our lives: decide, study, practice, teach.

1. Which discipline have you **decided** to address?

2. What will you need to **study** to learn it well?

3. How will you **practice** those truths in your life?

4. Who can you **teach** to follow in your example?

UNNOTICEABLY NOTICEABLE

*"Beware of practicing your righteousness before other people
in order to be seen by them" (Matt. 6:1).*

In the Sermon on the Mount, Jesus preached a sermon of which the world has yet to recover. In one section, he spoke of three spiritual disciplines that he assumed would be present in the lives of his disciples. Read Matthew 6:1-18 and write down which ones he emphasized.

#1 (6:2):   **#2 (6:5):**   **#3 (6:16):**

Jesus didn't isolate these disciplines for the super-spiritual elite. He didn't instruct us regarding "if" we would do them, but "when" we would do them. His underscored expectation reveals how he taught concerning each discipline's importance.

How did Jesus teach us to ensure that the audience for our spiritual disciplines was him and not others?

Our spiritual disciplines should be unnoticeably noticeable. We should never parade them around to impress others, but it should be evident that we are committed to them. Someone who is genuinely growing through these spiritual habits is never in need to prove to others of their activity. Their lives are the megaphone, and they need no introductions. The fruit that they provide is the noticeable difference. Pray that you will engage the disciplines for God's approval and not man's.

DISCIPLINE REVIEW

To review this week, how do you plan to initiate discipline in your Distinctive Discipleship plan?

Discipleship must train in certain areas of spiritual discipline for continual growth.

1. What spiritual discipline are you going to address next?

2. What do you hope this spiritual discipline will provide for your soul?

3. What lessons have you learned from someone who practiced this discipline well?

4. What type of plan will you begin to utilize?

PLAN NOTES

Category #5:

I will focus on the **discipline** of

What is my plan to experience progress in this area?

ESTABLISHING
DEPENDENCE

For it is God who works in you, both to will and to work for his good pleasure (Phil. 2:13).

Paul described discipleship in a complex way when he wrote, "For this I toil, struggling with all his energy that he powerfully works within us" (Col. 1:29). God's work and our efforts are both expected for our growth. In the last session, we studied the need for discipline as we toil for progress, but any successful improvement is due to God's power rather than our abilities. God is the means for our growth even when we use personal methods for our growth. In this session, we will study the last category regarding our dependence on God for successful discipleship.

CONSIDER

Who was your hero? We all had that person who seemed larger than life and untouched by mediocre abilities. Whether that person proved to have superior mental, physical, or practical skills, you felt mesmerized in their presence.

Who was your hero? What was his or her "superhero" power? Write it down and share it with the group.

Did the wonder of your hero inspire you to be better or discourage you from even making an attempt?

Heroes have a way of inspiring us or immobilizing us. That's what makes discipleship so complicated yet glorious. God is the undeniable hero. He does the work, but he also calls us to do part of the work. Some people expect God to do all the work, and we are not required to contribute anything to the process. Others claim that we are fully responsible for the outcome and leave God out of the equation. What is dangerous about both of these extremes?

What is the danger of refusing responsibility for our growth?

What is the trouble with assuming total responsibility for our growth?

In this session, we will discover that our dependence on God does not lead us to negligence but ambition. If you truly comprehend God's power to move, it should encourage you to engage even more diligently.

STUDY

In teaching the church of Philippi, the Apostle Paul highlighted the need for joy in the Christian life. Writing from within a prison cell, he knew firsthand the weight of that necessary perspective. Read his description of Jesus in Philippians 2:1-11.

How should focusing on the life of Jesus bring joy to our lives?

After this description, he introduces a thought that initially seems contradictory. Read Philippians 2:12-13 and write out the two seemingly competing thoughts about "work."

Describe the work in verse 12.

Describe the work in verse 13.

Apparently, we accomplish spiritual growth by our work that God works within us. So does our maturity happen due to our responsibility or God's activity? The answer is yes. It is both.

To help us grasp this truth, we must think through how we are to work out our own salvation in the first place. Since we know that we are not saved by our works (Eph. 2:9), what does it mean to work out our own salvation? Christ did the work by dying upon the cross (Phil. 2:8). The work remaining for us to do is discipleship. Our persistent efforts at spiritual growth prove that the gospel has truly changed us.

When you received the gospel, you experienced justification when God declared you not guilty. As you continue through discipleship, you are experiencing sanctification as God continues to work on you through his means and your efforts.

What are tangible ways to work out one's salvation?

Among that type of effort, what does it mean that God is working in your work?

Why is it significant that God sees our personal growth as related to his "good pleasure?"

DISCUSS

God working through our work is a common theme throughout the Bible. Get volunteers to read the following verses or read them together. As you study them, write words or phrases down beside the reference that shows the nature of God's work in our lives.

Psalm 16:1-2	**Rom. 12:3**
1 Cor. 4:7	**Heb. 13:21**
2 Cor. 4:7	**1 Cor. 12:6**
2 Chron. 30:12	**1 Cor. 15:10**

God's Word reminds us that we are dependent upon his power for spiritual growth, but that truth should never lead us to laziness. Paul knew his spiritual positioning was due to God's grace, and yet that caused him to work harder than anyone else (1 Cor. 15:10). God's activity should never lead us to immobility. We are dependent upon his efforts but never sidelined by them.

How should our dependence upon God elevate our personal efforts?

Why do we struggle to believe that God can do incredible things in our lives?

We often perceive God to work differently now than he did in the Bible. **Why do you think we act as if God has retired from the miraculous?**

God has not retired from the ministry. His years of work has not limited his present capabilities. The God who created the world, parted the Red Sea, shut the mouths of lions, and brought the dead back to life is the same God to whom you pray. Maybe the reason we aren't seeing God do anything in our lives is that we aren't expecting it.

When is the last time you recognized God as on the move in your life?

As you share these moments as a group, realize the point of the last question. The event you shared is not the last time God did something, but it might be the last time you recognized it. We are dependent upon God for so much of which we are so unfortunately unaware.

EVALUATE

It is time to get specific. In your Distinctive Discipleship plan, what are you dependent upon God to do? While we know he is the power behind all spiritual successes, what are you uniquely presenting before him in need of his strength?

> *What then shall we say to these things? If God is for us, who can be against us? He who did not spare his own Son but gave him up for us all, how will he not also with him graciously give us all things (Rom. 8:31-32)?*

Do you believe that God is for you? Really? Do you envision God eager for you to succeed in your spiritual growth?

A confident belief that God wants to move in your life is vital for your discipleship. If God is for our growth, who can be against it? You might think of a few different candidates. While nothing should be able to succeed against us, many things, unfortunately, hinder our spiritual growth and development. **In your honest assessment, what are the things working against your growth right now?**

Regarding your growth right now, what is entirely out of your hands? What must be a matter of prayer? Think of items within your control (what you must prayerfully ask God to assist in your efforts) and those outside your control (those things of which you are entirely dependent).

WITHIN   **OUTSIDE**

SHARE

Regarding your growth, what are you dependent upon God to do? Share an item from each list for which you will be actively praying.

Remember that our dependence upon God should increase our activity and not diminish it. God is for you. He is with you. He empowers you. Your efforts are magnified due to the power he works within you. Pray for one another regarding the specific issues that you shared.

SESSION NOTES

If you are reading the **Distinctive Discipleship** book to accompany this study, read **chapter 10** before coming to the group next time.

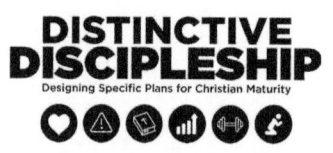

WHEN THE HELP STOPPED

And his fame spread far, for he was marvelously helped, till he was strong
(2 Chron. 26:15).

In the Old Testament, God's people knew the difference that a godly or an ungodly king could make. Authors archived key events in the lives of the many kings spanning numerous generations. By way of introduction, these accounts often provided a summary statement indicating the overall spiritual direction of their lives and leadership. Regarding King Uzziah, his narrative included a rare occurrence when the archivist spoke well of his administration at first yet shared a tragic decision at the end of his life.

Read what changed in Uzziah in 2 Chronicles 26:1-23. **What caused the dramatic turnaround in Uzziah's life?**

Uzziah had initially sought God (26:5), experienced prosperity (26:5), and received help (26:7). "As long as he sought the LORD, God made him prosper" (2 Chron. 26:5). The problem for him was that his many successes led him to a dramatic downfall. "He was marvelously helped until he was strong. But when he was strong, he grew proud, to his destruction" (26:15-16).

The moment we think we don't need God is when we need him most of all. How desperately dependent on God are you? Remember that pride goes before destruction (Prov. 16:18). You have been marvelously helped up to this point in your life. Don't confuse your past advances as a guarantee for future accomplishments.

MISPLACED FAITH

*And Jesus said to him, "'If you can!' All things are possible
for one who believes" (Mark 9:23).*

As you begin to ask God to do the things of which you are unable, you must develop a necessary level of faith. You shouldn't display arrogance in your abilities, but you should maintain confidence in God's power. How confident are you in God's ability to do the miraculous? A certain man approached Jesus with rightly-directed faith even though it was underdeveloped. Read about the event in Mark 9:14-29.

Jesus had already given his disciples authority over unclean spirits (Mark 6:7), but they were unable to address this specific situation (Mark 9:18). Mere association with Jesus doesn't guarantee access to his power. Just because the disciples had previously been victorious did not mean they could work from their own strength. We will always lose spiritual battles if we rest on previous accomplishments or personal abilities.

This father did come to the right person, but he wasn't coming to him in the right way. His audacious remark represents so many of us. Do it, Jesus, if you can. Our lack of faith often robs us of seeing Jesus work miraculously in our lives. Jesus can do whatever he wants. All things are possible for the one who believes.

While the disciples and the father responded in different ways, both parties revealed misplaced faith. The father was unsure Jesus could do it, and the disciples assumed that they could do it. **Which one do you identify with more? Why?**

OUR GOD IS ABLE

"If this be so, our God whom we serve is able to deliver us from the burning fiery furnace, and he will deliver us out of your hand, O king" (Dan. 3:17).

When God exiled his people to Babylon, they had to learn how to live for God in a land that did not. While many succumbed to the pressures of the pagan nation, some young men defied the odds and remained faithful amidst persecution. Three young men vowed not to worship the king even if it led to their death. Read about their ordeal in Daniel 3:8-30.

Shadrach, Meshach, and Abednego showed steadfast resolve to stay faithful to their God regardless of the outcome. They exhibited a peaceful trust knowing that God could save them even if he didn't.

What makes their response so unique (Dan. 3:16-18)?

Do you have some circumstance of which you know that God could fix it but unsure if he will? How should that alter your prayers?

Who do you think was the fourth man in the fire (3:25)? Who are the options?

How have you seen God's constant presence amidst your trials?

PRAYERFUL PERSPECTIVE

And now, O Lord, for what do I wait?
My hope is in you (Ps. 39:7).

When David was overwhelmed with God's discipline in his life, he maintained a proper perspective and took his concerns to God through prayer. Too often we talk to everyone else before talking to God. Sometimes we actually ask others to pray for a situation more than we pray for it ourselves. **When trouble comes, who do you usually go to first?**

Read David's approach in Psalm 39:1-13.

How did David's perspective of his life's longevity affect the way he thought about his condition (39:4-7)?

Our lives are too fleeting to overwhelm ourselves with trivial issues. Since we are characterized by brevity and frailty, we should focus on matters more for their eternal implications rather than their temporal inconveniences. David considered us as sojourners (Ps. 39:12). We are only travelers passing through. You probably have a legitimate prayer list today, but are you praying with eternity in mind?

Write out your major prayer concerns today and process through what God-glorifying results would look like in your life. After you write them out, call out to God in prayer and remind yourself of your utter dependence upon him.

ANXIOUS FOR NOTHING

Do not be anxious about anything, but in everything by prayer and supplication with thanksgiving let your requests be made known to God (Phil. 4:6).

As a prisoner incarcerated for the crime of doing God's work, Paul knew firsthand the perseverance needed for following Jesus. He encouraged the church in Philippi to rejoice in their circumstances. Aware of the uncertain times awaiting them, Paul encouraged these people dear to his heart. Read some of his final instructions in Philippians 4:4-7.

Why do you think Paul repeated his instruction to rejoice in the Lord (4:4)?

When circumstances confront us and tempt us to worry, we cannot ignore them or hope they will simply go away. We must commit to prayer. Don't let anything cause you to worry but let everything cause you to pray. In Phil. 4:6, Paul uses the term "prayer" and "supplication." "Prayer" is the general term for talking with God. "Supplication" refers to the specific requests made.

Why do you think thanksgiving is needed during these particular times of prayer?

We tend to resort back to anxiety and attempt to take matters into our own hands. God's Word is clear – we must fight against stress and depend on prayer. **Why do you think Paul says that the peace of God after prayer can guard both heart and mind? Which do you need more?**

DEPENDENCE REVIEW

To review this week, how do you plan to establish dependence in your Distinctive Discipleship plan?

Discipleship must continually acknowledge the complete dependence upon Jesus for the believer's maturity.

1. What are you praying for God to do that only he can do?

2. What are you praying for God to do through you regarding what he expects only you to do?

3. Where do you believe yet still struggle with unbelief? What would you publicly declare he can do but privately wonder if he will do?

4. Is your plan specific enough to determine if you see success or not?

PLAN NOTES

Category #6:

My prayers of **dependence** will ask God to

How will these prayers be specific and gaugeable?

IMPLEMENTING
DISCIPLESHIP

*Practice these things, immerse yourself in them,
so that all may see your progress (1 Tim. 4:15).*

Over the last seven sessions, you have narrowed down expansive lists of general discipleship needs to personal discipleship steps. Even though you haven't implemented the entire process yet, hopefully, you are already beginning to see some growth. In this last session, you will put all the pieces together and initiate your plan. While you have experienced progress, now it is time to define your distinctive strategy which you will use for the months to come.

CONSIDER

While we all came to this study in a different spiritual place, and we will each leave with a different set of directions, we have all benefitted from the insight and encouragement from others. Your story encouraged another's. Your steps in the past helped direct another's decisions in the future.

How have you been encouraged by the progress seen in others during this study?

Proverbs 27:17 says that we are to sharpen one another. **What is one way that this group has sharpened you during this study?**

What thought has made the most significant impact on you as we have designed your specific plan for Christian maturity?

We all joined the group in unique situations. We will all leave with distinct plans. God has used the assembling together to produce love and good deeds in one another (Heb. 10:24-25). In today's session, we will help one another put the finishing touches on our Distinctive Discipleship plans and begin the process. The real power of this study will not be experienced in the passing of information but afterward in the practice of implementation.

STUDY

Before we embark upon this journey of discipleship, we must count the cost of such a trip. The manner of completion will be proportional to the level of preparation.

Read Jesus' words on discipleship in Luke 14:25-27.

What is the most shocking suggestion by Jesus?

How would you explain that concept to someone more immature in the faith?

In Jesus' culture, "hating" was an expression of loving something less based on a comparison. Other biblical examples employ this language to make a statement on the placement of priority rather than an example of vindictiveness (Gen. 29:30-31; Matt. 10:37).

What does it practically look like to place your commitment to Jesus above all other relationships?

When Jesus spoke of taking up a cross (Luke 14:27), it was before he died upon his. **What would those original disciples have understood Jesus to mean at that moment when he instructed them to take up their cross?**

Now read his words in Luke 14:28-33.

How is discipleship like building a tower (14:28-30)?

How is discipleship like waging war (14:31-32)?

Each of us must count the cost to follow Jesus. We need more than motivation to begin; we need preparation to endure. If not careful, we will finish this session with high aspirations yet fail to follow through due to a lack of planning.

DISCUSS

Since today marks the day that you implement your complete plan, we must help one another prepare for success. **Why do you think many disciples fail even when they have good intentions?**

What is your greatest danger? Are you worried you will try to accomplish too much or attempt too little?

Completing your Distinctive Discipleship plan means that you are going to select at least one issue for six categories to address for the months to come. As a way to ensure that everyone in the group truly understands each type, let's review them one more time.

> To them God chose to make known how great among the Gentiles are the riches of the glory of this mystery, which is Christ in you, the hope of glory. Him we proclaim **[Delight]**, warning everyone **[Disobedience]** and teaching everyone with all wisdom **[Doctrine]**, that we may present everyone mature in Christ **[Development]**. For this I toil **[Discipline]**, struggling with all his energy that he powerfully works in me **[Dependence]** (Col. 1:27-29).

Within your group, briefly discuss the meaning of each category.

1. What does **delight** have to do with discipleship?

2. What do we mean by **disobedience**?

3. What is **doctrine**?

4. How would we define **development**?

5. What does **discipline** mean in the Christian life?

6. How does a Christian reveal **dependence**?

As you have collected ideas for your plan, now is the time to solidify what makes it on the list and identify next steps.

EVALUATE

This section might require you to turn to earlier pages. You will rewrite your goals a few times as a way to reinforce them in your mind. While this process can take eight weeks to unpack, if it isn't simple enough to write on a notecard, you have made it too complicated.

For the next few months, what will your Distinctive Discipleship plan be?

		Reference
1.	I need to **delight** in Jesus more than	Page 41
2.	My **disobedience** that must be addressed is	Page 57
3.	The pivotal **doctrine** for me to study is	Page 73
4.	I need **development** in learning how to	Page 89
5.	I will focus on the spiritual **discipline** of	Page 105
6.	My prayers of **dependence** will ask God to	Page 121

After you complete each sentence, write out some notes under each one of the necessary steps or helpful resources. Think through these items.

- Is there a resource I need?

- Is there a wise mentor I need to seek?

- What are the next steps?

- How will I know if I have been successful?

After you have finished making your notes, use the worksheet in the back of this book to fill out a single page guide as you go forward. The goal is that you know these six items so well that you can tell them to another if someone asks you.

SHARE

One of the best ways to start our distinct plans is to share them with encouraging people. Take some time for each of you to read your complete proposal to one another. You can be as thorough as time allows. At the very least, read a few categories from your six statements that define your plan.

Before this session ends, the most important gift you can give to one another is accountability. Each of you needs to share one more piece of information: Who will walk beside you during this process? This model will be good for an individual, better with a partner, but best with a mentor. **Who will be with you?**

Take some time to pray for one another. Be specific in your prayers regarding the distinct plans of those around you. After you say "amen," the study concludes, but the journey actually begins.

SESSION NOTES

If you are reading the **Distinctive Discipleship** book to accompany this study, read **chapter 11** as you complete your plan.

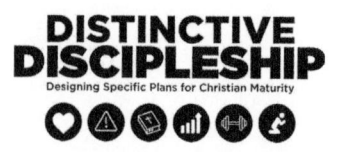

WHO ARE YOU?

But the evil spirit answered them,
"Jesus I know, and Paul I recognize, but who are you?" (Acts 19:15).

Whenever a believer advances in discipleship, supernatural forces are aware. While the inhabitants of heaven rejoice, the agents of hell seek retaliation. Many believers will know some information about Satan, but does Satan know about you?

During Paul's missionary journeys, we read an account that contains a description of demons that might surprise you. Read Acts 19:11-20.

These traveling Jewish ministers did not believe in the name of Jesus, but they were trying to use the name of Jesus for their own personal advancement. **What does their defeat teach us about such a strategy?**

The demons obviously knew Jesus, but they were also fully aware of a missionary named Paul. He had done enough damage to their kingdom to garner their attention. What about these seven sons of Sceva? These imposters weren't even on Satan's radar. No one posted memos about their imposing danger. No one showed concern regarding their power. This example begs the question: do the forces of hell know you by name?

From this passage, it appears that the forces of hell have a list of humans that pose a threat to their activity. They have enemies. Are you one of them? Have you considered that some of your opposition over these last few weeks might be due to their efforts in response to your progress? Pray to put on the full armor of God to stand firm in times of looming battles (Eph. 6:12).

DAY 2: INVESTIGATE
UNBURDENED OBEDIENCE

For this is the love of God, that we keep his commandments.
And his commandments are not burdensome (1 John 5:3).

As you have completed your Distinctive Discipleship plan, you have selected a focus for both the delight and disobedience category. While all six types are related to one another on the path of discipleship, these two are uniquely connected. The more that we delight in Jesus, the less appealing disobedience will be. If we find joy in the paths of the Word, we will lose interest in the ways of the world. So avoiding sin should not be a burden but rather a blessing. Look how John described it in 1 John 5:1-5.

How does loving the Father relate to loving others (5:1-2)?

Why do we often feel as if obedience is a burden (5:3)?

In your life, what commandments did you at one time consider a burden?

More than offering God a miserable state of submission, we desire to reach a point where we obey for sheer joy. Why would we even consider another path over his? Pray that God would begin to shape your affections. Pray that you would seek obedience out of desire rather than duty. Find his ways as an opportunity more than an obligation.

132   DISTINCTIVE DISCIPLESHIP BIBLE STUDY

DAY 3: IMITATE
IT'S TIME TO GROW UP

When I was a child, I spoke like a child, I thought like a child, I reasoned like a child. When I became a man, I gave up childish ways (1 Cor. 13:11).

In the third and fourth categories of your Distinctive Discipleship plan, you highlighted ways to grow in the areas of doctrine and development. The more that you study biblical information, the more that you will experience biblical transformation. The truths in your head will eventually make it to your hands. The Apostle Paul spoke to the need to grow up in our faith. Within a section when he taught the Corinthians on the roles of spiritual gifts (1 Corinthians 12-14), we read a popular text focusing on love. While many read this passage in varying contexts, the actual setting of this content in the Bible is related to how we develop in our gifting for the benefit of the local church. Read his description in 1 Corinthians 12:27-14:1.

Why is love an essential consideration for how we use our spiritual gifts?

Paul taught that he had matured throughout his life. In what ways have you grown (13:11)?

How will your focus on doctrine and development cause you to grow up?

UNABLE TO GO BACK

And it was told King David, "The LORD has blessed the household of Obed-edom and all that belongs to him, because of the ark of God" (2 Sam. 6:12).

In the fifth and sixth categories of Distinctive Discipleship, you have selected a focus in the areas of discipline and dependence. The frequency and quality of your spiritual disciplines can often indicate the level of dependence you have on God. In the Bible, a certain worshiper was thrust into a daily communion with God that forever altered his state of dependence. As King David prepared to bring the Ark of the Covenant back into Jerusalem, something shocking occurred. They neglected to obey the instructions of how to transport the ark, and God punished a man named Uzzah to get their attention (2 Sam. 6:7). Read what happened in 2 Samuel 6:1-15.

After the frightening reminder of God's judgment, David instructed a relatively unknown priest named Obed-Edom to take responsibility for the ark. Living ten miles outside the city, he moved this critical piece of Israel's history into his home. After three months of reported blessing, David wanted proximity to the ark again, but this time, he obeyed biblical instructions (2 Sam. 6:13).

A subtle yet powerful part of the narrative is tracking what Obed-Edom does next. When the Bible begins to list the people in charge of caring for the ark and ministering in the temple, Obed-edom's name is listed repeatedly. He serves as a worship leader (1 Chron. 15:21), gatekeeper (1 Chron. 16:38), and minister (1 Chron. 26:4, 12-15). This committed volunteer lived ten miles away but could care less about the trouble of such travel. Why? Once someone truly experiences the presence of God, he or she can never settle for less again.

How do you see your disciplined actions causing you to depend on God more?

DON'T GROW WEARY

And let us not grow weary of doing good,
for in due season we will reap, if we do not give up (Gal. 6:9).

This week you have implemented your Distinctive Discipleship plan. You have completed the difficult task of narrowing down an expansive list of possibilities to a doable guide for your maturity. In addition to beginning your process, a worthy goal is to complete it as well. Along the way, you might grow weary in this important yet challenging work. Read the words of the Apostle Paul in Galatians 6:1-10 to draw from a reliable source of strength.

Why does Paul say that we need to bear one another's burdens (6:2) yet bear our own parts (6:5)?

How does Paul's instructions on sowing and reaping intersect your Distinctive Discipleship plan (6:7-8)?

What words in Galatians 6:9 are the most-needed reminders for you?

What measures have you taken to ensure that you don't give up along the way? If you don't have them in place, now is the time. Write them down and pray over them as you begin.

DISCIPLESHIP REVIEW

To review this week, have you thoroughly planned to begin your Distinctive Discipleship plan?

If there is a true profession of faith, there should be a true progression of faith.

1. Is there any area of your plan that still needs more focus?

2. Why do you think the plan will be successful?

3. Are you worried that you will fail? Why do you feel that way?

4. What systems of accountability have you put in place to set yourself up for success in the coming months?

PLAN NOTES

SESSION 8: IMPLEMENTING DISCIPLESHIP   137

DISTINCTIVE DISCIPLESHIP

RESOURCES

In the following pages, you will have some examples as well as some worksheets to fill out. You can use these to fill out your personal guide or as a place to keep track with someone you are discipling.

You can access digital copies of these worksheets and additional resources at **travisagnew.org/distinctive**.

CATEGORY EXAMPLES

In case you struggle with selecting a focus for each category, here are some samples to acclimate your mind to the type of selection you need to make.

DELIGHT - I need to **delight** in Jesus more than

- The approval of others
- Staying busy for Jesus
- My favorite sports team
- My physical appearance
- Obeying commandments out of fear

- My spouse's happiness
- Finding a spouse
- My home and possessions
- My children's success
- My favorite hobby

DISOBEDIENCE - My **disobedience** that must be addressed is

- Alcoholism
- Greed
- Fits of anger
- Pornography
- Unwholesome speech

- Racism
- Bitterness
- Flirtatious ways
- Consistent lying
- Stealing from work

DOCTRINE - The pivotal **doctrine** for me to study is

- The Gospel
- Marriage & Sexuality
- The Holy Spirit
- Election
- Old Testament Overview

- The Second Coming
- Image of God
- Deity of Christ
- The Trinity
- The Role of Scriptures

DEVELOPMENT - I need **development** in learning how to

- Share my faith
- Love my spouse
- Discern and use my spiritual gifts
- Address my finances
- Teach a Bible study

- Time management
- Disciple my children
- Be a better church member
- Improve my physical health for the glory of God
- Do my job better

DISCIPLINE - I will focus on the spiritual **discipline** of

- Bible Reading
- Prayer
- Scripture Memory
- Fasting
- Worship

- Giving
- Sabbath rest
- Service
- Evangelism
- Church Involvement

DEPENDENCE - My prayers of **dependence** will ask God to

- Calm my anxiety
- Reconcile my family
- Save my friend
- Raise the money needed for missions
- Restore the joy of his salvation

- Make me patient
- Heal my neighbor's sickness
- Send more workers to the harvest
- Bring unity in our church
- Soften my spouse's heart

DISTINCTIVE DISCIPLESHIP

Designing Specific Plans for Christian Maturity

Name: John Smith

DELIGHT - *Christ in you, the hope of glory*

I need to **delight** in Jesus more than the approval of others.

ACTION PLAN

Research verses on my identity in Christ	I will avoid social media every Saturday	Find a way to give credit to a co-worker once a week

DISOBEDIENCE - *warning everyone*

My **disobedience** that must be addressed is greed.

ACTION PLAN

Memorize 10 verses on danger of greed	Give 12% of my gross income to the church	Volunteer at homeless shelter once a month

DOCTRINE - *teaching everyone with all wisdom*

The pivotal **doctrine** for me to study is the Holy Spirit.

ACTION PLAN

Journal notes from studying all Spirit passages in Bible	Ask pastor to recommend 3 best books on Holy Spirit	Acknowledge Holy Spirit in morning prayers

DEVELOPMENT - *present everyone mature*

I need **development** in learning how to teach my group better.

ACTION PLAN

Watch online courses on how to teach the Bible	Design feedback survey for 3 members in group	Record myself teaching and force myself to listen

DISCIPLINE - *for this I toil*

I will focus on the spiritual **discipline** of Scripture memory.

ACTION PLAN

List out first 25 verses I need to memorize	Research and select system to keep track of verses	Ask Steven to make me recite verses to him weekly

DEPENDENCE - *struggling with all his energy*

My prayers of **dependence** will ask God to reconcile my family.

ACTION PLAN

I will pray for my family daily by name	I will initiate contact with each member once a week	I will do my part to live at peace (Rom. 12:18)

Start Date: August 18

Estimated End Date: June 1

Who Will Evaluate: Randy my small group leader

When to Evaluate: Lunch every other Wednesday

DISTINCTIVE DISCIPLESHIP

Designing Specific Plans for Christian Maturity

Name:

DELIGHT - *Christ in you, the hope of glory*
I need to **delight** in Jesus more than

ACTION PLAN

DISOBEDIENCE - *warning everyone*
My **disobedience** that must be addressed is

ACTION PLAN

DOCTRINE - *teaching everyone with all wisdom*
The pivotal **doctrine** for me to study is

ACTION PLAN

DEVELOPMENT - *present everyone mature*
I need **development** in learning how to

ACTION PLAN

DISCIPLINE - *for this I toil*
I will focus on the spiritual **discipline** of

ACTION PLAN

DEPENDENCE - *struggling with all his energy*
My prayers of **dependence** will ask God to

ACTION PLAN

Start Date:

Who Will Evaluate:

Estimated End Date:

When to Evaluate:

DISTINCTIVE DISCIPLESHIP

Name:

Designing Specific Plans for Christian Maturity

DELIGHT - *Christ in you, the hope of glory*

I need to delight in Jesus more than

ACTION PLAN

DISOBEDIENCE - *warning everyone*

My disobedience that must be addressed is

ACTION PLAN

DOCTRINE - *teaching everyone with all wisdom*

The pivotal doctrine for me to study is

ACTION PLAN

DEVELOPMENT - *present everyone mature*

I need development in learning how to

ACTION PLAN

DISCIPLINE - *for this I toil*

I will focus on the spiritual discipline of .

ACTION PLAN

DEPENDENCE - *struggling with all his energy*

My prayers of dependence will ask God to

ACTION PLAN

Start Date:

Estimated End Date:

Who Will Evaluate:

When to Evaluate:

DISTINCTIVE DISCIPLESHIP

Name:

Designing Specific Plans for Christian Maturity

DELIGHT - *Christ in you, the hope of glory*
I need to **delight** in Jesus more than

ACTION PLAN

DISOBEDIENCE - *warning everyone*
My **disobedience** that must be addressed is

ACTION PLAN

DOCTRINE - *teaching everyone with all wisdom*
The pivotal **doctrine** for me to study is

ACTION PLAN

DEVELOPMENT - *present everyone mature*
I need **development** in learning how to

ACTION PLAN

DISCIPLINE - *for this I toil*
I will focus on the spiritual **discipline** of

ACTION PLAN

DEPENDENCE - *struggling with all his energy*
My prayers of **dependence** will ask God to

ACTION PLAN

Start Date: Who Will Evaluate:

Estimated End Date: When to Evaluate:

DISTINCTIVE
DISCIPLESHIP

Name:

Designing Specific Plans for Christian Maturity

DELIGHT - *Christ in you, the hope of glory*

I need to **delight** in Jesus more than

ACTION PLAN

DISOBEDIENCE - *warning everyone*

My **disobedience** that must be addressed is

ACTION PLAN

DOCTRINE - *teaching everyone with all wisdom*

The pivotal **doctrine** for me to study is

ACTION PLAN

DEVELOPMENT - *present everyone mature*

I need **development** in learning how to

ACTION PLAN

DISCIPLINE - *for this I toil*

I will focus on the spiritual **discipline** of

ACTION PLAN

DEPENDENCE - *struggling with all his energy*

My prayers of **dependence** will ask God to

ACTION PLAN

Start Date:

Estimated End Date:

Who Will Evaluate:

When to Evaluate:

DISTINCTIVE DISCIPLESHIP

Designing Specific Plans for Christian Maturity

GROUP GUIDE

NAME	 DELIGHT	 DISOBEDIENCE	 DOCTRINE	 DEVELOPMENT	 DISCIPLINE	 DEPENDENCE

DISTINCTIVE DISCIPLESHIP
Designing Specific Plans for Christian Maturity

GROUP GUIDE

NAME

DELIGHT

DISOBEDIENCE

DOCTRINE

DEVELOPMENT

DISCIPLINE

DEPENDENCE

DISTINCTIVE DISCIPLESHIP
Designing Specific Plans for Christian Maturity

GROUP GUIDE

NAME	 DELIGHT	 DISOBEDIENCE	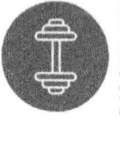 DOCTRINE	 DEVELOPMENT	 DISCIPLINE	 DEPENDENCE

DISTINCTIVE DISCIPLESHIP
Designing Specific Plans for Christian Maturity

GROUP GUIDE

NAME

 DELIGHT

 DISOBEDIENCE

 DOCTRINE

DEVELOPMENT

DISCIPLINE

 DEPENDENCE

For more resources, visit
travisagnew.org/distinctive.

Printed in Great Britain
by Amazon

35621887R00088